EXPLOSION OF PEOPLE EVANGELISM

By

DONALD C. PALMER

MOODY PRESS

CHICAGO

TO
my brothers and fellow-laborers
for Christ in Colombia
and
my wife, Dorothy

© 1974 by
THE MOODY BIBLE INSTITUTE
OF CHICAGO

Library of Congress Catalog Card Number: 73-15087

ISBN: 0-8024-2413-9

Printed in the United States of America

Contents

Illustrations

Tables

Foreword

Solomon said, "Of making many books there is no end; and much study is a weariness of the flesh," and I have agreed with him repeatedly. But reading the manuscript of this book by my friend and associate, missionary Don Palmer of the Gospel Missionary Union, was not a weariness to either my flesh or spirit. I found it intriguing, informative, and provocative. Mr. Palmer has written with unusual objectivity about the relative growth of the various Protestant churches and groups in Colombia. And what he has written about Colombia applies to most of the Latin American countries.

The author has certainly studied his subject thoroughly, sincerely, and with genuine objectivity. One detects that he sought for himself the secret of the very rapid growth of certain groups working in his field, and his analysis leads to some inevitable conclusions.

Certain groups of Colombian churches are recognizably growing much more rapidly than others. Does this mean that God is blessing these certain groups more than others? Is it because of a particular doctrine, or doctrines? Is it because of emphasis on personal experiences? Is it that these certain people are more zealous and more spiritual than others? Or, do methods of procedure and organization enter into the church growth? This book, I think, pinpoints the answer.

Of course the author does not agree doctrinally with some of the groups to which he attributes numerical success in Colombia. Nor do I. But he obviously made his study of the situation with openness and honesty and has drawn his analysis

9

in the same spirit and with evident objectivity. His conclusion is that we can learn from sound methods employed even by bodies that hold what we do not consider sound doctrine.

Numerical growth alone in national churches is not enough. But it cannot be denied or forgotten that numerical growth is a part of church growth, as is evidenced in the New Testament and in church history. True church growth must embrace soul-winning and membership addition, internal cohesion and stability, doctrinal soundness, and a biblically oriented and instructed congregation.

No one will seriously read this book without profit.

G. Christian Weiss

Preface

Colombia, as all of Latin America, is in the throes of change and transformation. New things are happening in this country which has been known as the most traditional, Spanish, and Roman Catholic of Latin America. Once the scene of the devastating *"La violencia,"* and the accompanying persecution of Evangelicals, Colombia is now witnessing a rapidly growing Protestant church and rapidly expanding opportunities for evangelism and church planting.

Yet, not all evangelical church groups are experiencing growth, and some are experiencing far greater church growth than others. Why is this? What are the major factors in the growth of these expanding churches? And what implications does their growth have for other evangelical denominations and missions in Colombia and Latin America? These are the concerns of this book.

To find the answers to these questions, I interviewed over two hundred pastors, leaders, and church members in Colombia over a period of three years. I also took the opportunity, whenever possible, for firsthand observation of church meetings and activities, especially those of the most rapidly growing congregations.

Three cities were chosen as case studies: Bogota, Pereira, and Palmira. In these three cities, pastors and leaders were interviewed, and there was opportunity for direct observation of meetings and activities in a number of local churches. Most of the members interviewed were in Pereira and Palmira, due to the greater problem of distance, time, and expense involved in the Bogota aspect of the study.

There were three main reasons for choosing these cities as case studies: (1) they represent fields of varying degrees of responsiveness to Protestant efforts; (2) I have a closer knowledge of Protestant work in these cities than in many others; (3) each city differs from the others in many ways. They are located in different sectors of the country, have different topography and climate, vary in population and racial structure, and express many regional differences in dress, speech, means of livelihood, and local customs. This gives the opportunity to test Pentecostal church growth with people living under somewhat differing circumstances and environments within Colombia.

This book is intended to aid us who serve in evangelical churches and missions, as we seek to evaluate our own ministries, and as we plan our strategy for carrying out the Great Commission in this and other countries of Latin America. Ultimately, the objective is that it help to lead and inspire us to greater church growth and multiplication.

The original title of this book, my master of arts thesis, "The Growth of the Pentecostal Churches in Colombia," describes the nature, emphasis, and locale of this investigation. It is a church-growth study, focused on Colombia, South America, where I was a missionary with the Gospel Missionary Union from 1959 to 1971. The emphasis is upon the growth of the Pentecostal churches and the principal reasons for this growth.

This study considers several basic questions: (1) how great is the growth of the Pentecostal churches in Colombia, as compared to that of other non-Pentecostal Protestant churches there; (2) what are the distinctive beliefs of these Pentecostal churches; (3) what are the principal factors in their growth; and (4) what implications does their growth have for other Protestant denominations working in Colombia and Latin America?

The last two questions are the most important for us in this investigation. In examining *why* the Pentecostal churches are growing as they are, I have sought to find the methodological, sociological, and doctrinal factors which have contributed to this growth. Then I have evaluated and analyzed this growth by pointing out what could be considered negative aspects in Pentecostal growth, as well as by emphasizing those positive factors in their growth which can teach us important lessons, and guide us to greater church growth in the non-Pentecostal denominations of Colombia and other countries of Latin America.

METHODS OF INVESTIGATION

Three major methods of investigation were employed in gathering information for this work: the study of written materials; interviews with church leaders, pastors, and members; and direct observation of church services and meetings.

The written materials included: (1) books and articles on the Pentecostal movement in general, its beginnings, history, distinctive beliefs; (2) books and articles on the philosophy of missions, missions strategy, and church growth, especially Pentecostal church growth in Latin America; (3) books and articles dealing with sociology and religion in Colombia and Latin America; and (4) Pentecostal publications, periodicals, manuals, constitutions, tracts, and other materials produced and used by the Pentecostal denominations in Colombia.

Three questionnaires were prepared to guide the majority of the interviews. (The complete text of these questionnaires can be found in the Appendix.) The questionnaire for directors required an interview of approximately one to two hours, and was aimed at getting a general picture of the denomination: its history, growth, methods of evangelism and church planting, institutional ministries, methods of leadership preparation for ministries in the churches, and so on.

The questionnaire for pastors was the longest and most detailed of the three questionnaires, and required an interview of two to three hours. The focus in this case was on the local church: its beginnings, growth, methods of outreach, leadership, standards, and so on. A brief supplement was added to the basic questionnaire for interviews with non-Pentecostal pastors and leaders, concerning their observations on the Pentecostal churches and their methods and growth.

The questionnaire used with church members was designed to answer questions such as: by what means were the majority of members interviewed won to Christ; what kind of people does Pentecostalism attract; what do many people find in the Pentecostal churches that they do not seem to find in other Protestant churches; what makes Pentecostals more active witnesses; and how do the members of different denominations view education and community involvement?

Two methods were employed with this questionnaire—the individual and group approaches. In the case of the fastest growing churches, I sought to get a sampling of interviews with individual members. With other churches—both Pentecostal and non-Pentecostal—I arranged for group interviews with members, usually at a midweek service. The groups were purposely kept small, generally between ten to twenty members made up a group. Only the questions considered to be the most important in the questionnaire were asked in the case of group interviews.

This questionnaire was designed for a shorter interview time than those for pastors and directors, and could be completed in an hour or less.

On several occasions, invitations to speak or take part in Trinitarian Pentecostal church services presented good opportunities for firsthand observation of their meetings: who directed, how the meetings were carried out, what opportunities there were for participation by the members, the enthusiasm and spirit manifested during the service, and so on.

Besides these opportunities, I also attended several meetings in unitarian Pentecostal churches (Jesus Only), as an observer. Since these churches had a large attendance, my presence did not seem to call undue attention, and I felt that the services were carried out in a normal way.

The principal denominations represented in this study, which have local churches in at least two of the three case-study cities, can be listed in two groups—the Pentecostals and the non-Pentecostals.

The Pentecostals include: (1) the Assemblies of God; (2) the Panamerican Mission; and (3) the United Pentecostal Church, also known as the Jesus Only church (UPC).

The Non-Pentecostal churches include: (1) Southern Baptist; (2) Cumberland Presbyterian; (3) Christian and Missionary Alliance (CMA); and (4) the Gospel Missionary Union (GMU).

Other denominations that are represented only in the overall statistical picture, and in the Bogota study, are the Worldwide Evangelization Crusade (WEC), Interamerican Church (founded by the Oriental Missionary Society), United Presbyterian Church, Mennonite General Conference (MGC), International Church of the Foursquare Gospel, and the Church of God.

As I see it, this study has three limitations. First, not all Protestant denominations are represented. Sects such as the Mormons and Jehovah's Witnesses are not included at all. Neither is special mention made of the Seventh Day Adventists. Other Protestant denominations that do not have local churches in the three case-study cities may be mentioned only in the overall statistical comparison of Protestant churches in Colombia. And in Bogota, which has so many churches of different denominations, only the most representative for the case study were chosen for interviews.

The second limitation is the problem of statistics. For instance, some denominations and churches keep almost no records of membership or attendance. This is especially true of the Jesus Only Pentecostal churches. Nevertheless, on the basis of the pastors' calculations and personal observation, I have sought to achieve a fairly close approximation to the true figures.

Also, even when records are kept, pastors and local churches are sometimes careless about assuring *accurate* statistics. In some cases, only rough estimates of membership and attendance have been available, especially for the earlier years.

Another problem with statistics is that the requirements for baptism and membership vary between denominations. For example, one church or denomination may show many more members than another, but have lower standards for membership. If both had the same standards, the growth picture would be somewhat modified.

Most of these statistical limitations are, of course, applicable to all church-growth studies. These limitations do not, however, change the fact that comparisons and trends can be definitely established despite some inaccuracy.

A third limitation the reader must realize is that the situation in a local church is never static. Conditons change continually in a local congregation. A change of pastor or leadership can often bring rapid church growth, or loss. Spiritual renewal, new outreaches, and special efforts can change the growth trend of a local church. As a result, some of the conclusions drawn in earlier investigations may later prove to be somewhat obsolete. This is especially true since a full schedule in the ministry in Colombia made it necessary for me to gather materials for this survey over an extended period.

At the same time, the extended-time factor had some value. Some conclusions that I might have drawn after a brief study of several months, were proven inaccurate and omitted. Others had the opportunity to confirm themselves.

Recognizing the above limitations, this study is offered with the hope that it may help us in evaluating our own ministries and churches in Colombia and Latin America, and that it may assist us in planning our strategy for missionary work in this continent for the coming years.

Acknowledgments

Dr. David Hesselgrave and Dr. Herbert Kane, two of my professors in the School of World Mission of Trinity Evangelical Divinity School, have given me invaluable advice and encouragement from the beginning of this work. The directors of the Gospel Missionary Union, the mission board with which I am presently serving, and especially its president, Rev. R. J. Reinmiller, have contributed by giving me the go-ahead to take the necessary time from other duties to finish this investigation.

In Colombia itself, many have contributed by sharing with me the information I needed. It would not be feasible to list all of their names here, but I would like to mention the help received from the denominational directors, pastors, missionaries, and church leaders with whom interviews were held, and whose information has contributed to the findings presented in this study. Because of the extra time and information they have given me, I would especially like to acknowledge the help of Glen Kramer, past supervisor of the Assemblies of God in Colombia; of Ignacio Guevara, founder and principal leader of the Panamerican Mission; and of Rev. Domingo Zuniga, past director of the United Pentecostal Church in Colombia. Others who gave their time and counsel were Eugene Kelly of the Christian and Missionary Alliance, Dr. George Biddulph of the Interamerican Mission, and Ray Zuercher of the Gospel Missionary Union.

Then, Dr. James Goff, secretary for the Evangelical Confederation of Colombia for many years, made the confederation's statistical files available to me. Dr. Alan Neely, professor at the Southern Baptist Seminary in Cali, directed a committee of his denomination in a Baptist church growth study, and shared some of the results of this study with me. Then I should mention Ed Murphy, Ruperto Velez, and Donald Fults, of Overseas Crusades in Colombia. Their understanding of church-growth principles and their overall view of Protestant work in Colombia, made the information and opinions they shared with me invaluable for this book.

Finally, I acknowledge the contribution of Trinity Evangelical Divinity School, and of the Evangelical Free Church which sponsors it, to my further preparation through its school of World Mission.

1

Socio-Religious Background of Colombia

Colombia is the fourth largest nation in South America, both in size and population. Its land area is approximately equal to that of the combined states of Texas and California.[1] Nevertheless, about 98 percent of the people are concentrated in the western third of the country, and most of these in the fertile mountain valleys, high temperate plateaus, and along the northern Atlantic coast. As a result of migration to the urban areas, over half of the people now live in the cities, as compared to only 35 percent in 1940.[2] Racially, the people consist of white, Negro, Indian, and mestizos—a mixture of these races.

The population of Colombia, as of Latin America as a whole, is increasing rapidly. In 1947, the population of Colombia was estimated at a little over 10,500,000.[3] In 1970, just twenty-three years later, the population had more than doubled, to over 21,000,000.[4] The present annual growth rate of the population is 3.4 percent,[5] and if this rate continues, by 1980 the population will be almost 30,000,000! This represents a great responsibility for us of the evangelical churches of Colombia.

Roman Catholicism has been the predominant religion in Colombia since the sixteenth century, when it was colonized by Spain. In 1967, the Roman Catholic church claimed 17.9 million members out of a total population of 18.7 million, or 96 percent![6] One sociological study states that "in effect, in the mind of nearly all of the people, to be a Colombian is to be

19

a Catholic."[7] Roman Catholicism has been woven into the culture and customs of the people to the point where, for many, to be a patriotic Colombian, one must give at least nominal loyalty to the church.

> In Colombia, it is almost axiomatic that the controlling force in society is the Roman Catholic Church. There is no segment of life, no daily activity which is not affected by the ubiquitous presence and influence of the Church. Nowhere in Latin America does the Church enjoy the prestige and power of religious monopoly as it does in Colombia. The oft-heard expression "to be a Colombian is to be a Catholic" is more than idiomatic. To leave the Church then is interpreted not only as an act of heresy, but treasonable as well.
>
> It should not be concluded that such an absurd idea is as widely held in Colombia today as it was a generation ago. The scene is radically and extensively changing. The Church, nevertheless, will not apparently sacrifice ungrudgingly its favored position. The Concordat is still appealed to by clergy and politician alike. The Liberal Party President, Carlos Lleras Restrepo, in the last few days has again consecrated the country to the Sacred Heart of Jesus. . . . Even after an unbelievable amount of liberalization, the Roman Catholic properties still are the only ones universally exempt from taxation. In most communities evangelicals pay taxes even on their buildings of worship.[8]

Colombia *is* changing, and likely will continue to change, becoming less and less intolerant toward the Evangelicals and their ministries. And while Colombia is still considered to be strongly Roman Catholic, especially in some areas of the country, it is also true that today "there is widespread nominalism and only an estimated ten percent of the Catholic membership is considered acitve."[9]

It is also important to note that the baptismal archives of the Roman Catholic church are the official records of birth in the nation. This greatly increases Catholic membership statistics, without indicating whether these claimed members are in any way active in the church. Indeed, some leaders within the

Catholic church admit that the majority of its members is nominal only, taking almost no *active* part in the life or activities
of the church. Speaking of Latin America in general, James
Fonseca, editor of *Catholic Notices,* states that although 90
percent of the population in Latin America is baptized, not
more than 30 percent of these ever take first communion.[10] In
Colombia, the trend to nominalism within the church can be
seen in the city of Cali, as noted by a priest from there.

> In Cali, Father Hurtado Galvez recently stated that in an
> average week no more than 50,000 people attend mass in
> this city of more than 800,000. Thus, according to Hurtado,
> a little more than 6% of the population is involved weekly in
> this basic activity of the Church.[11]

So while the percentage of Colombians that have been baptized in the church, and consider themselves Catholics, is very
high, the number that faithfully attend and participate in the
mass, and that regularly receive the sacraments, is a small percentage of the total membership.

EARLY PROTESTANT EFFORTS

Protestant missionary work began in Colombia in 1825 with
the colportage efforts of a Bible society agent. The Presbyterian Church, USA, established the first permanent ministry
in the country in 1856, and in 1865 received the first Colombian believers as members in Bogota. This marked the beginning of the first Protestant church in Colombia. Protestant activities, however, were very limited during these early years.[12]

The second Protestant mission to enter Colombia was the
Gospel Missionary Union, a member of the Interdenominational Foreign Mission Association (IFMA), in 1908. The
GMU pioneered in the western part of Colombia, introducing
the gospel and the Bible in innumerable towns and cities in the
western states, called *Departamentos.* Other Protestant missions did not enter until 1925 and later. Some of these earlier
Missions were the Christian and Missionary Alliance, which
entered in 1925; the Cumberland Presbyterian, in 1927; and

the United Pentecostal Church in 1936. Protestant Churches grew on a very limited scale up to this time, and in 1937 it was estimated that the baptized Protestants represented approximately 0.02% of the total population in Colombia. This would mean that there were about 1,800 Protestant church members in that year—certainly a small number!

1940—1960

In the subsequent period, between 1940 and 1960, Protestant church growth began to increase in Colombia, and other Protestant missions entered the country. Some of these were: the Southern Baptists and the International Church of the Foursquare Gospel, in 1942; the Interamerican Mission and the Mennonite General Conference, in 1943. The Panamerican Mission, an indigenous church, came into being in 1956.

Many Protestant churches suffered a great deal of persecution during the period between 1949 and 1959, a time of political civil war known as *La Violencia* (the violence). The dispute, which was between the two principal political parties, took on religious overtones as well, and Protestants were severely persecuted in many areas by fanatical Roman Catholics. "Hundreds of cases of imprisonment, and even martyrdom of evangelical believers and the destruction of Protestant church buildings and other properties took place during this time."[13] The church which suffered the greatest loss of members was the Gospel Missionary Union, which had concentrated much of its efforts in some of the areas hardest hit by *La Violencia*. According to annual statistics taken from the GMU's monthly periodical in Colombia, *El Mensaje Evangelico,* the number of members dropped from 1,015 in 1948, to 513 in 1950, as a result of the persecutions. Most of the members that were lost were people that were forced to flee to safer places, where the GMU did not have local churches. In a number of places, local churches ceased to exist, as some members were killed and the others fled. And what the GMU experienced during this time of violence, the other Protestant churches also experienced in varying degrees.

Despite the persecution, however, Protestant membership increased significantly, from 7,908 in 1948, just before the violence began, to 33,156 in 1960, at the end of this period of persecution. This represented more than a fourfold growth.[14]

1960—1970

The past decade has witnessed a great change in the religious climate in Colombia. While fanaticism and intolerance still exist, especially in some rural areas and in the traditionally stronger Roman Catholic centers, the religious freedom that most Evangelicals enjoy today is unprecedented in the history of this country. Liberalization and change have taken place in the thinking of the leaders of the country, as well as in the Roman Catholic church itself. This is due in part to the effects of the Vatican Council II and the influence of Pope John XXIII. It may also be due in part to the bad publicity the Catholic church received as a result of atrocities committed in her name against the Protestants during the decade of violence. The church was anxious, no doubt, to change her image before the public.

As a result of these changes, the Protestant churches have greater opportunities today than ever before in Colombia. Open-air meetings are held in many places where before this was unknown. Many commercial radio stations that previously refused to allow evangelical broadcasts now sell time quite freely for these programs in the major cities. The reading of the Bible is encouraged by some of the Catholic prelates, and Evangelicals have even been given the opportunity to teach the Bible and show gospel films in some of the Catholic schools and colleges. This is a new day of opportunity for the Protestant churches in Colombia.

This past decade has also witnessed the greatest Protestant church growth in Colombia. The census of CEDEC (the evangelical confederation of Colombia), taken in 1960, reported 33,156 baptized members, and a total Protestant constituency of 165,780.[15] This, of course, is a small number when compared to some of the other Latin American countries. In

1960 it was calculated that in all of Latin America, "there were 6,150,000 in the Protestant community out of a total population of 180,000,000. Thus, on an average, the Protestants then comprised approximately 3.4% of the population, whereas in Colombia the ratio of 1.2% was much lower."[16] This means, of course, that the total Protestant church in Colombia is relatively small. But it is the *rate* of growth that we are primarily interested in. The latest Protestant census is that of CEDEC for 1969. According to this census, total membership has increased from 33,156 in 1960, to 90,573 in 1969.[17] This means that it multiplied by almost three times in nine years! And though still representing a small total number, Protestant membership, as a percentage of the population, increased from 0.23 to 0.44 during this same period, despite the fact that the population also increased significantly. The total Protestant constituency in 1969 was estimated at 271,719, or 1.3 percent of the population—still not very large, but showing a definite increase.[18]

But then we note something else which is very significant, and which we will see in the next chapter: while the Protestant church as a whole is experiencing good growth in Colombia, the Pentecostal churches are outstripping other Protestant denominations in their *rate* of growth. And once we have shown that the Pentecostal churches are the fastest growing in Colombia, we have established the importance of finding the reasons for their superior growth.

THREE CASE STUDIES

In the preface, I mentioned that each of the case-study cities differs from the others in many ways. It is important to get at least a brief picture of the social and religious background of each of these cities.

Bogota is the capital, and also the largest city in Colombia, with a population of over two million people. Located in the department of Cundinamarca, on an extensive plateau over 8,000 feet in elevation, Bogota is the political, cultural, and educational center of the country.

Racially, the people of Bogota are Spanish white and mestizo, a mixture of Indian and white. The Chibcha Indians were the earliest inhabitants of this part of Colombia, and their influence can still be seen in many of the people here. The majority of the people live in the popular suburbs, called *barrios,* most of them made up of the lower classes. Many of the wage earners from these *barrios* work in factories, on construction jobs, and in transportation (as bus, taxi, and truck drivers). Others have their own small trades and stores.

As far as Protestant efforts go, Bogota represents a moderately open field, especially in recent years. Evangelicals have liberties as never before in radio, open-air meetings, and visitation. Nevertheless, intolerance and opposition to Protestant efforts are not unknown, especially in certain sectors of the city.

The Presbyterians began their work in Bogota many years before the other missions, but their growth has been limited. The Pentecostals have had the greatest growth, especially the Assemblies of God. It is here that the Assemblies have had their greatest success in Colombia. Consequently, the concentration of interviews in Bogota was with the Assemblies of God.

Pereira lies west of Bogota across two ranges of the Andes Mountains and the Magdalena Valley. With a population of 250,000, it is one of three important cities in what is known as the Caldas region. (The other two cities are Manizales and Armenia.) Recently the new department of Risaralda was formed, with Pereira as its capital. The city has a reputation for being civic-minded and progressive, and is a hub for commerce, transportation, and education in this part of the country. Since coffee is the principal mover of the economy in this area, many work in the cultivation, picking, processing, and sale of this commodity. Others work in the many small, locally owned factories and businesses which characterize this region, and in several large, foreign-controlled companies.

Of the three case-study cities, Pereira has the highest proportion of Spanish white people. Nevertheless, an Indian influence can be seen in many. Pereira became one of the many "cities of refuge" during *La Violencia,* when thousands of people fled the surrounding rural areas for the comparative safety of the city. Because of this, Pereira became known as "The City of Open Doors."

Roman Catholicism traditionally has been stronger in the Caldas-Antioquia region of Colombia; and for this reason, Pereira has been a semiresistant field, though this is changing. Until recent years, the Protestant churches were quite restricted in opportunities to use commercial radio or conduct open-air services. With the large influx of new people during and after *La Violencia,* and with the new spirit of tolerance in Roman Catholicism, some of the fanaticism toward Evangelicals has disappeared. Nevertheless, most of the Protestant churches have grown very slowly here, and others are either standing still or have actually lost ground. The most notable exception to this is the United Pentecostal Church, which has achieved very strong growth. Following them in growth, but quite a ways behind, is the Panamerican Mission, an indigenous Pentecostal denomination which is similar in beliefs to the Assemblies of God.

Palmira, with a population of 120,000, is the smallest of the three case-study cities, and is located south of Pereira in the southern part of the Cauca Valley. It is largely an agricultural center, since it is surrounded by some of the richest and most productive farmland in the nation. In some respects, Palmira is also a satellite of the city of Cali, eighteen miles away, with a population of almost one million. Cali is the industrial center in this part of Colombia. In Palmira, the Negro influence is much stronger than in Bogota or Pereira. There are the Spanish white, Negro, and those that are largely Indian, but the majority of the people are a mixture of these racial groupings. Many of the people in Palmira work in the huge sugar refineries and canefields on the outskirts of the city, and others work in factories and small businesses in Palmira and in Cali.

Palmira has been a more open field for Protestant efforts for many years. Gospel work has a fairly long history here, and the people have generally been less fanatic than in Bogota or Pereira. In fact, the biggest complaint of some of the Protestant pastors and leaders in the city is that many of the people are indifferent to religion of any kind—Roman Catholic or Protestant.

The oldest and most established work in Palmira is that of the Gospel Missionary Union, but it has suffered losses in membership in its churches in recent years. The Cumberland Presbyterian church is still very small and is barely growing. The strongest church, in terms of membership and growth, is again the United Pentecostal, or Jesus Only, Church. No other denomination comes close to it in the number of members. Of the non-Pentecostal churches here, the Southern Baptist has had the steadiest growth, and stands second in membership to the United Pentecostal Church, though it is much smaller.

All three of these case-study cities—Bogota, Pereira, and Palmira—have this in common: the Pentecostal churches are growing much faster than the rest of the Protestant denominations. Our concern in this study is to find the reasons for this. In the following chapter, we will give a statistical picture and comparison of church growth in Colombia, and in the case of the three cities, some of the background of this growth.

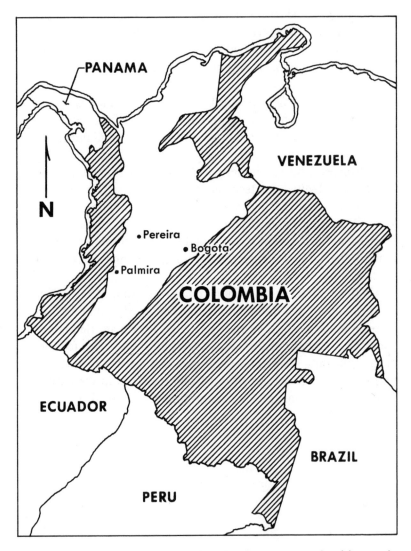

Fig. 1. Map of Colombia showing the three case-study cities, and
         the most populated area of the country (in white)

2

Statistics of Church Growth in Colombia

Today, Pentecostalism is the fastest-growing Protestant movement in Latin America. The various Pentecostal churches now claim more adherents than all the other Protestant denominations put together. According to a recent Latin American church-growth study, the Pentecostal churches accounted for 63 percent of the total Protestant membership of Latin America in 1969. Their growth has been especially strong in countries such as Chile, Brazil, Mexico, Venezuela, and El Salvador.[1]

The same trend can be seen in Colombia. The Pentecostal missions began here later than many of the other Protestant denominations, and by 1960 accounted for 16 percent of the total Protestant membership.[2] Nine years later, this had increased to just under 40 percent.[3] At this rate, the Pentecostal churches may, in the fairly near future, have more than 50 percent of all Protestant church members in Colombia. The fact that the Pentecostal churches are increasing their percentage of the total Protestant membership in Colombia is all the more significant when we realize that the Protestant churches as a whole are experiencing a very good growth here.

GENERAL OVERVIEW

For a better comparison of membership and growth between the Pentecostal and non-Pentecostal denominations, four categories may be formed: (1) Pentecostal churches, (2) Denominational churches (churches founded by denominational missions), (3) Faith mission churches (churches founded by interdenominational faith missions), (4) Seventh-day Adventist churches.

It is revealing to note the growth trend of each of these categories of churches in recent years. (In the following tables, all numbers are from 1970 unless otherwise indicated.) In table 1, membership growth of these churches is noted for the period from 1960—1969. Several things can be noted from this comparison. The Pentecostal churches have had the most rapid growth, having multiplied over six times in nine years. They have grown over twice as fast as the faith mission churches, about three times as fast as the Adventist churches, and their rate of growth has been almost ten times that of the denominational churches.

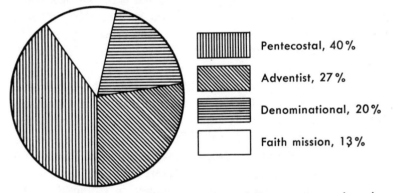

Fig. 2. Types of churches: Percentage of Protestant members in 1969. (SOURCE: *Census of Protestant Church Members: 1969,* pp. 3-5.)

As a group, the faith mission churches have had the best growth of the non-Pentecostal denominations. They almost tripled their membership in this period, a much better growth rate than that of the denominational churches.

CHURCHES INCLUDED IN THIS STUDY

We shall now become more specific, and compare the growth and ministries of the individual churches most involved in this study. These would include the denominations whose leaders

TABLE 1

<small>Types of Churches: Members and Percentage Growth,</small>
1960—1969

	1960	1969	Growth
Pentecostal churches	5,396	35,653	560%
Adventist churches	11,866	24,828	110%
Denominational churches	11,478	18,748	60%
Faith mission churches	4,416	11,344	160%
Total	33,156	90,573	

<small>Source: *Census of Protestant Church Members: 1969,* pp. 3-5.</small>

were interviewed and that had local churches in at least one of the three case study cities. The one exception to this is the Foursquare church.† For the purpose of making their identification easier, the churches are divided into four groups: (1) traditional denominations; (2) faith mission churches; (3) Trinitarian Pentecostal; and (4) Unitarian Pentecostal.

Membership

We shall begin by comparing the membership growth of these churches for the ten-year period from 1960 to 1970. From table 2, we note that among the smaller denominations (100—1,000 members in 1960), most of them experienced good growth, but the Panamerican and Assemblies of God churches had the greatest growth. The Panamerican church membership increased by thirteen times, and the Assemblies of God membership by ten times!

Among the larger denominations (over 1,000 members in 1960), the Christian and Missionary Alliance was the only non-Pentecostal church to more than double its membership, with a growth of 131 percent. Yet the Foursquare church grew even more (145 percent growth), and the United Pentecostal Church had *by far* the greatest growth, multiplying its membership by ten times! With an estimated 30,000 members in

† The Foursquare church does not have churches in these cities but is included because of its size and importance.

TABLE 2

YEARS OF PREACHING IN COLOMBIA, AND MEMBERSHIP GROWTH FROM 1960—1970

	YEAR FOUNDED IN COLOMBIA	YEARS OF PREACHING	MEMBERS IN 1960	MEMBERS IN 1970	PERCENTAGE INCREASE
Group 1					
United Pres.	1856	114	1,684	2,760	64%
CMA	1925	45	1,571	3,644	131%
Cumberland Pres.	1927	43	859	1,238	44%
Southern Baptist	1942	28	3,422	5,383	57%
Mennonite	1943	27	143	277	94%
Group 2					
GMU	1908	62	764	1,492	96%
WEC	1933	37	692	1,717	148%
Interamerican	1943	27	588	1,723	193%
Group 3					
Assemblies of God	1942	38	159	1,580	900%
Foursquare	1943	27	1,524	4,300 (1969)	145%
Panamerican	1956	14	105	1,400	1,230%
Church of God	n.d.	?	219	719	230%
Group 4					
UPC	1936	34	3,000	30,000	900%

SOURCE: Statistics for this and the following tables are taken from three sources: (1) the statistical records and census of CEDEC; (2) official yearly denominational reports; and (3) figures given me in interviews with denominational leaders.

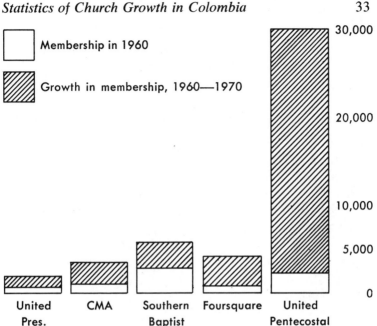

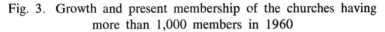

Fig. 3. Growth and present membership of the churches having
more than 1,000 members in 1960

1970, it is now the largest Protestant denomination in Colombia.

Of course, membership figures do not give a completely accurate picture, since the requirements for membership vary between denominations. Some groups, such as the Southern Baptist, Gospel Missionary Union, Assemblies of God, and the Panamerican Mission, claim twice as many believers as baptized members. On the other hand, the Cumberland Presbyterian and the United Pentecostal churches have an almost equal number of believers to baptized members in their churches, the UPC because they strongly emphasize baptism almost immediately after conversion. So they do not have many believers that are not baptized members. If all the churches practiced this, the membership of some would more than double, and that of others would at least increase significantly. This would *somewhat* modify the growth picture, and the United Pentecostal membership growth would be some-

TABLE 3

GROWTH IN NUMBER OF LOCAL CHURCHES FROM 1960—1970;
AVERAGE MEMBERSHIP AND ATTENDANCE PER
LOCAL CHURCH

	CHURCHES IN 1960	CHURCHES IN 1970	AVERAGE MEMBER-SHIP	AVERAGE ATTEND-ANCE
Group 1				
So. Baptist	30	56	96	191
CMA	24	54	67	85
United Pres.	21	34	81	113
Cumberland Pres.	9	10	124	128
Mennonite	3	5	56	87
Group 2				
GMU	17	42	36	80
WEC	14	28	50	81
Interamerican	?	35	50	86
Group 3				
Foursquare	23	68 (1968)	63	89
Assemblies of God	3	53	28	72
Panamerican	4	40	35	100
Church of God	6	16	45	102
Group 4				
UPC	43	400	75	94

what less marked in comparison to that of the other denominations. Nevertheless, the fact remains: the United Pentecostal
Church has experienced the greatest growth of any Protestant
church in Colombia.

NUMBER OF LOCAL CHURCHES

Not only is it significant to compare membership growth, it
is also important to see which denominations are most successful in multiplying local churches. Again, we are comparing
only the churches most involved in this study.

The statistics from table 3 show us some interesting facts.
In most cases, the denominations which have the highest
growth rate in membership are also the ones that are multiply-

ing local churches the fastest. In the period from 1960 to 1970, the Assemblies of God, Panamerican Mission, and the United Pentecostal Church, all increased the number of local churches by ten times or more; the Foursquare and Church of God by almost three times.

It is also significant to note that the CMA, which has experienced the greatest membership growth among the larger non-Pentecostal denominations, also had the greatest increase in the number of local churches in this group. On the other hand, the Cumberland Presbyterian church, which has had the lowest rate of membership growth among the denominations we are studying, also had the least increase in the number of local churches, adding only one church in ten years! This stands in contrast to the United Pentecostal Church, which claims 357 new churches in this ten-year period; the Assemblies of God with fifty new churches; and the Panamerican Mission, with thirty-six.

The average size of the local churches, in terms of membership and attendance, varies a great deal between the different denominations. The Assemblies of God has the lowest average membership and attendance per local church, while the Cumberland Presbyterian has the highest average membership, and the Southern Baptist the highest average attendance per local church.

The Pentecostal Jesus Only churches are the most widespread geographically in Colombia. Of the twenty-six *Departamentos,* they claim churches and preaching points in twenty-two of them. Other denominations which are quite widespread in Colombia are the Southern Baptist, CMA, and Assemblies of God.

PASTORS AND LEADERS

One of the main aims in missions and in building local churches is to recognize and train national leaders. A strong national church cannot be built without strong national leadership; and when churches are multiplied, leaders must also be multiplied in number. Table 4 gives a statistical picture of the

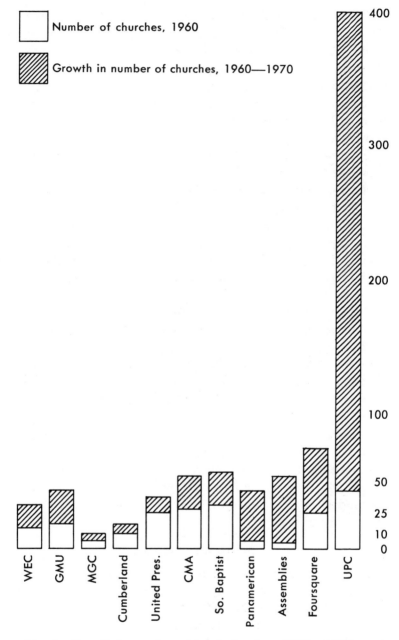

Fig. 4. Growth in number of local churches, 1960—1970

number of pastors, ordained and nonordained, that were serving in different denominations in 1970. The ratio of members per pastor, and the number of missionaries serving in each denomination is also noted.‡

The denominations with the largest number of pastors, both ordained and nonordained, are the United Pentecostal Church, Foursquare, Assemblies of God, Southern Baptist, and the Panamerican Mission.

Churches with the highest ratio of nonordained pastors to ordained pastors are the Assemblies of God, United Pentecostal, Interamerican, and Panamerican Mission. This means that the Pentecostal churches, as a whole, have the highest

TABLE 4

NUMBER OF PASTORS AND MISSIONARIES; RATIO OF MEMBERS
TO PASTORS IN THE DIFFERENT DENOMINATIONS

	ORDAINED		NON-ORDAINED	TOTAL	MEMBERS/ PASTOR	MISSION-ARIES
Group 1						
So. Baptist	36		24	60	1/90	53
CMA	18	(1971)	60	78	1/51	33
United Pres.	22		12	34	1/81	6
Cumberland	4		11	15	1/83	8
Mennonite	2		3	5	1/56	10
Group 2						
GMU	10		24	34	1/42	18
WEC	15		5	20	1/50	21
Interamerican	6		25	31	1/56	25
Group 3						
Foursquare	50	(1968)	55	105	1/35	7
Assemblies	7		53	60	1/25	10
Panamerican	10		40	50	1/28	7
Church of God	?		?	26	1/28	. .
Group 4						
UPC	70		310	380	1/80	4

‡The UPC and Panamerican churches are both indigenous churches which have no formal ties with foreign mission boards. The missionaries that work with them are not directly affiliated with them, but are independent missionaries that co-operate with their churches.

number of pastors, *and* the highest ratio of nonordained to ordained pastors. Many of these nonordained pastors are lay pastors in charge of local congregations.

The Assemblies of God, Church of God, and Panamerican Mission churches have the lowest member-to-pastor ratio of all denominations. We have already mentioned the low aver-age membership per local church in these Pentecostal churches. This shows us something of the church-planting and leadership strategy of these churches, and we will refer to this in a later chapter.

The missions with most missionaries in Colombia are the Southern Baptist, Christian and Missionary Alliance, and the Interamerican Mission. Missions with the highest ratio of mis-sionaries to members are the General Conference Mennonite

TABLE 5

CHRISTIAN DAY SCHOOLS AND STUDENTS

	PRIMARY	SECONDARY	TOTAL SCHOOLS	TOTAL STUDENTS
Group 1				
United Pres.	26	5	31	3,800[a]
Southern Baptist	28	1	29	2,209
CMA	23	3	26	700
Cumberland Pres.	4	1	5	802
Group 2				
GMU	9	0	9	540
WEC	20	1	21	565
Interamerican	13	1	14	1,305
Group 3				
Foursquare (1967)	6	0	6	469
Assemblies of God	5	1	6	?
Panamerican	4	0	4	?
Church of God	8	0	8	272
Group 4				
UPC	10[b]	0	10	?

[a]Estimate based on the number of students in 1966 and the number of schools in 1970 as compared to 1966.

[b]The director of the UPC could not give an exact figure, but estimated there were about 10 primary schools.

and the Interamerican Missions. Both have a high proportion
of missionaries in institutional work. The United Pentecostal
and Panamerican churches are indigenous, and consequently
have practically no foreign missionaries working with them.
Besides these, the missions with the *least* foreign missionaries
in comparison to membership, are the Foursquare, Assemblies
of God, and United Presbyterian.

INSTITUTIONS

CHRISTIAN DAY SCHOOLS

It is clear from table 5 that the denominations which have
put the most emphasis on Christian day schools are the United
Presbyterian, Southern Baptist, Interamerican, and Cumberland Presbyterian. The United Presbyterian Church has more
students in its schools than members in its churches, while the
Cumberland Presbyterian and Interamerican churches have
about two-thirds as many students in their day schools as members in their churches. The United Presbyterian Church sponsors the most schools of any group, with thirty-one, and has
almost as many schools as churches (thirty-four).

The denominations which have the least schools in comparison to membership are the Pentecostal groups. The United
Pentecostal Church has put the least emphasis on education.
and has just a few schools among its four hundred churches.

THEOLOGICAL SCHOOLS

A number of the denominations in this study have no residence schools for theological training, while others have a
strong emphasis in this area. The Southern Baptists have a
large international seminary in the city of Cali, and the Interamerican Mission operates an interdenominational seminary in
Medellin, as well as a practical Bible institute for those who
have had very modest schooling. The Christian and Missionary
Alliance and the Worldwide Evangelization Crusade sponsor
Bible institutes for the training of their pastors, and the CMA
also has a practical Bible institute for training Indian believers.
In this kind of a school, the student divides his time between
study and work.

Among the Pentecostal churches, the Assemblies of God and Foursquare put strong emphasis on their Bible institute training programs for the training of their pastors, while in the Panamerican Mission and the United Pentecostal Church, few of the pastors have had any formal theological preparation. These churches rely primarily on short-term training institutes held periodically for their pastors and leaders.

TABLE 6

THEOLOGICAL SCHOOLS

	LOCATION	TYPE OF SCHOOL	NUMBER OF STUDENTS	SCHOOL TERM
Group 1				
So. Baptist	Cali	Seminary	56	9 mos.
CMA	Armenia	Institute	25	6 mos.
CMA	Silvia[a]	Institute	35	6 mos.
Group 2				
WEC	Bogota	Institute	50	6 mos.
Interamerican	Medellin	Seminary	16	9 mos.
Interamerican	Cristalina[a]	Institute	80	6 mos.
Group 3				
Foursquare	Bucaramanga[a]	Institute	103 (1967)	?
Foursquare	Barranquilla	Institute	12 (1967)	?
Assemblies	Bogota	Institute	75	6 mos.

[a]These are practical Bible institutes.

Some of the denominations that do not have their own residence theological schools, such as the Presbyterian and the Gospel Missionary Union, either send students to the seminaries and Bible institutes sponsored by other denominations, or use what is termed the seminary extension program. This is an autodidactic system using programmed texts, which gives theological training to the students where they live and work. Once a week, a teacher or pastor meets with the students in a given area for a period of discussion concerning the week's lesson. A number of the denominations which have their own residence Bible institutes or seminaries, also use this system, especially for the training of lay leaders.

OTHER INSTITUTIONS

In table 7, we note which denominations sponsor hospitals, orphanages, bookstores, or printshops.

TABLE 7

OTHER INSTITUTIONS SPONSORED BY THE DENOMINATIONS
INCLUDED IN THIS STUDY

	HOSPITAL[a]	ORPHANAGE	BOOKSTORE	PRINTSHOP
Group 1				
Southern Baptist	1	. .	1	. .
United Pres.	. .	1	. .	. .
Cumberland Pres.	. .	. .	. .	. .
CMA	. .	. .	6	. .
Mennonite	. .	. .	1	. .
Group 2				
GMU	1	. .	2	1
WEC	1	. .	1	1
Interamerican	. .	. .	2	. .
Group 3				
Foursquare	. .	. .	. .	. .
Assemblies of God	. .	. .	. .	. .
Panamerican	. .	. .	1	. .
Church of God	. .	. .	. .	. .
Group 4				
UPC	. .	. .	. .	. .

[a]Denominations that sponsor medical dispensaries are the United Pres., CMA, GMU, WEC, and Interamerican.

From this table, it is clear that the Pentecostal churches definitely sponsor less of these institutions than do the non-Pentecostal denominations. Among the five Pentecostal denominations, only one—the Panamerican Mission—had one of the four institutions considered, a small bookstore.

Generally the faith missions have sponsored the widest variety of institutions. The Presbyterians have concentrated especially on Christian day schools, while the Christian and Missionary Alliance has emphasized bookstore ministries, as well as having two theological training schools. The Southern

Baptists have a hospital and bookstore, as well as the seminary and twenty-nine Christian day schools.

RADIO

Radio, of course, can be used as a direct means of evangelism and teaching the Word. It can also be an effective means to help build local churches, when the programs acquaint the public with a particular denomination or local church. All of the Pentecostal denominations interviewed make use of radio in strategic centers. The Panamerican Mission had seven weekly broadcasts in 1970, more than most denominations interviewed. One of the most popular evangelical broadcasts in Colombia is "The Voice of the Conscience," by Paul Finkenbinder, a member of the Assemblies of God. In larger cities, some of the Assemblies of God churches sponsor their own "live" broadcasts. All of the Jesus Only churches in the larger cities try to broadcast on local commercial radio stations. Generally, local talent is used for these broadcasts.

The non-Pentecostal churches that are making the most use of radio today are the Christian and Missionary Alliance and the Southern Baptist. The only non-Pentecostal denominations that had no radio broadcasts in Colombia at the time I interviewed them were the United Presbyterian, Cumberland, and the Worldwide Evangelization Crusade.

3

A Picture of Church Growth in Three Cities

BOGOTA

The first Protestant denomination to begin work in Bogota was the United Presbyterian, in 1856, and in 1865 the first evangelical church in Colombia was organized there by the Presbyterian missionaries. The second Presbyterian church in Bogota was not organized until 1952, eighty-seven years later,[1] and the third church was organized in the early 1960s. Presbyterian church growth has been slow, and the total membership of their three churches in Bogota has actually decreased slightly since 1965. Most of this loss took place in the central church, though it is now picking up again under the leadership of Dr. Robert Lazear. Dr. Lazear gives three main reasons for the previous loss of members in this church: (1) a number of members, including the pastor, were drawn into the political left; (2) much of the preaching became divisive, since it became political (a number of members left to attend other churches as a result); (3) to supplement his salary, the pastor went into business, and his time and concern were diverted from the ministry.[2]

A primary emphasis of the Presbyterian church, from the beginning, has been education. In 1870 the first Presbyterian day school was opened in Bogota, and in 1885 the Colegio Americano for boys began to function.[3] By 1966, the coeducational Colegio had over 1,000 students and a complete program, from kindergarten through the primary and secondary grades.

43

The next mission to enter Bogota was the Worldwide Evangelization Crusade, in 1933. WEC is an interdenominational mission with some holiness background, whose primary emphasis is on evangelism and church planting.[4] Nevertheless, WEC has a wide variety of ministries, as is the case with many of the faith missions, and in Bogota itself has three primary schools, a forty-bed hospital, a bookstore, and a printshop. Nearby, in Funza, there is the WEC Bible institute, with over fifty students.

WEC has had the best growth rate of the non-Pentecostal denominations in the capital city, and by 1971 had eleven organized churches there. This denomination also has experienced the greatest influence of Pentecostalism in a number of its churches, especially in Bogota. Ralph Hines, missionary field leader, explained: "There is quite an emphasis in some churches on Pentecostal doctrine and experiences. . . . The Eduardo Santos and Asuncion Churches are completely Pentecostal, and the Marco Fidel Suarez Church is going this way."[5]

Adelmo Chavez, who is a pastor of one of the WEC churches in Bogota which has become Pentecostal, is the chief Colombian leader in this movement within the WEC. He, and others, were very impressed by what they saw and heard in the faith-and healing campaigns held by Eugenio Jimenez in Bogota in the 1960s, and became convinced that the Pentecostals were right in their beliefs on healing, the baptism of the Spirit, and speaking in tongues. Since then, he has pushed for this within his own church and denomination, with encouragement from some of the other WEC pastors and missionaries that felt the same way:

> One of our missionaries has been moving gradually into Pentecostalism for many years. When he saw the success and growth of the Pentecostal groups, he became convinced that they had something that was needed; now he is a Pentecostal and believes in Pentecostal doctrine. . . . The head of the WEC Bible institute is from a Pentecostal church; so he also sympathizes with the movement.[6]

As to the possible effects this all may have within the WEC in Colombia, Rev. Hines continues,

> Within the WEC, we are possibly heading for a division over the Pentecostal issue. This year in January, we organized for the first time a WEC young people's movement. But in March when the time came for the first conference, . . . the three churches of south Bogota would not cooperate. This is to me a sign that there is a moving apart. . . . WEC is growing on all fronts, and the new liveliness has done some good in our churches and has made us all think. But we face extremes and possible division. I only hope we can come into some balance.[7]

I asked Rev. Hines if the churches with the Pentecostal emphasis were growing more than the other churches. His reply was,

> I don't think we can say that yet, because they are not growing as fast as they expected to, and the non-Pentecostal churches seem to be growing just as well. . . . It will take a revival of true victory and joy in the Lord to show that it doesn't depend on tongues and other Pentecostal manifestations to see growth and fruit.[8]

The Southern Baptists organized their first church in Bogota in 1950, eight years after they had begun missionary work in Colombia in the city of Barranquilla, on the Atlantic coast. By 1960, there were three Baptist churches in Bogota, and in 1970, four. The Baptists also have a bookstore in downtown Bogota and a radio broadcast, "The Baptist Hour." Entering Bogota was part of their overall plan.

> The early ministry called for a strong but not necessarily large missionary staff which would function as a balanced team working in evangelistic, medical, educational, and agricultural ministries, and in theological and secular education. A bookstore, hospital, and seminary were envisioned and later were established. The Foreign Mission Board and the Jarman Foundation made funds available for the building of impressive church buildings in the larger cities.[9]

The Southern Baptists follow the general strategy of entering the larger cities, beginning with a group of believers, and as soon as possible, building a large, central church building. From there, they work out to the surrounding suburbs within the city and to neighboring towns. And the results have not been bad: today they have the largest total membership of any non-Pentecostal denomination, except the Adventists.

The rest of the missions and churches did not begin efforts in Bogota until after 1950. Table 8 gives a picture of the history of Protestant efforts there as of 1971.

TABLE 8

YEARS OF PREACHING AND NUMBER OF LOCAL CHURCHES

	YEAR FOUNDED	NUMBER OF YEARS TO 1971	NUMBER OF CHURCHES 1960	NUMBER OF CHURCHES 1970
United Pres.	1856	115	2	3
WEC	1933	38	4	11
So. Baptist	1950	21	3	4
Interamerican	1952	19	1	4
UPC	1955	16	1	8
Assemblies	1955	16	2	17
Panamerican	1956	15	4	6
Church of God	1961	10	1	3
CMA	1961	10	1	1
Mennonite	1964	7	0	1
Body of Christ	1968[a]	3	0	6

[a]The group known as Members of the Body of Christ left the Panamerican Mission in 1968.

The greatest church growth in Bogota has taken place since 1960, and the church which has had the most outstanding growth is the Assemblies of God. Their work in Colombia really began in 1935 in the town of Sogamoso, about 150 miles from Bogota. The Presbyterians had made some efforts in Sogamoso in the 1920s, resulting in a small group of believers there, but due to lack of personnel, they established no permanent work.

Then in 1933, the Edward Wagners, independent missionaries that had come to Colombia from Venezuela, took over what there was in Sogamoso. By 1935, there was a small, functioning church, and soon after, a Christian day school was begun. Later, construction was started on a church building, school facilities, and missionaries' home, all on the same compound.[10]

In 1942, the church in Sogamoso voted to unite with the Assemblies of God, and from then on, the entire Sogamoso work came under their direction. This, then, was the first Assemblies of God church in Colombia, and this continued to be the center of *all* their activity in the country, with very minimal growth, until the midfifties.

> The Sogamoso work operated on a paternalism missions basis, and remained there for twenty years with minimal development. The church building, missionary house, and school were all on one compound. The church didn't really expand outside the compound; it was a little American church in Colombia. The songs, form of service, and even the church building were North American. The church is still somewhat stymied in growth, though there are no missionaries there now. . . . This was the center of all Assemblies of God activity till the midfifties.[11]

Then, in 1955, a missionary couple with the Assemblies of God came to Bogota to begin work there. They were the Harry Bartels, who formerly were missionaries with the Mennonite Brethren in Colombia, but later were convinced of Pentecostal beliefs, and subsequently affiliated with the Assemblies of God. The Bartels aimed first to establish a strong church in the southern part of Bogota, then another in the north, and from these two churches to branch out to the surrounding *barrios*.

The south church, known as Bethel, was founded in 1956, and the north church in 1959. By 1966 these two churches had multiplied to six, by 1968 to twelve, and in 1971 to seventeen, and this does not include a number of other churches planted in towns near Bogota. This means that in the city itself, fifteen new churches were founded in fifteen years—an average of one new church every year!

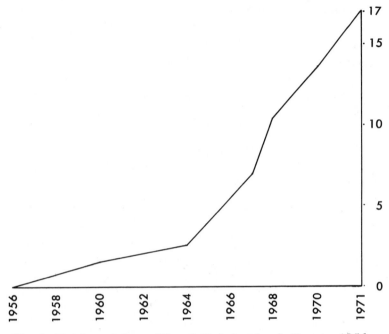

Fig. 5. Number of Assemblies of God churches in Bogota, 1956—
1971

In membership, the Assemblies of God is the largest church in Bogota, with slightly over 1,000 members in 1971. The United Pentecostal Church follows with over 900 members, but the requirements to become a member are higher in the Assemblies of God than in the Jesus Only churches. While the Assemblies claim over 2,500 average total attendance in their Bogota churches, the United Pentecostals claim 1,480.

From table 9, it can be seen that of the seven largest churches in Bogota, five are Pentecostal. If the trend of the past ten years continues in this city, the future is certainly bright for Pentecostal church growth. On the other hand, the denominations which have had the least percentage growth in membership in Bogota are the Presbyterian, Interamerican, and the Christian and Missionary Alliance.

Several denominations, especially Pentecostal, have suffered heavy losses from church splits in Bogota. In the midfifties,

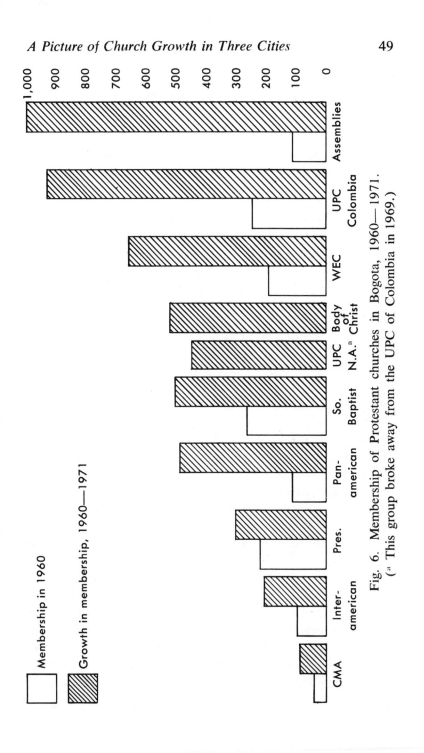

Fig. 6. Membership of Protestant churches in Bogota, 1960—1971. ([a] This group broke away from the UPC of Colombia in 1969.)

Membership in 1960

Growth in membership, 1960—1971

TABLE 9

MEMBERSHIP OF PROTESTANT CHURCHES IN BOGOTA,
1960—1971

	1960		1966	1971
Assemblies of God	106		293	1,005
UPC, Colombia	250		689	928
WEC	190		255	674
Body of Christ	..		..	520
Southern Baptist	265	(1961)	472	503
Panamerican	105		279	473
UPC, North America	..		..	447
United Pres.	225		333	305
Interamerican	80		122	191
Church of God (Pent.)	12		52	93
CMA	10	(1961)	30	70
Church of God of Prophecy[a]	..		..	56

SOURCE: Data is from the CEDEC census, denominational records, and figures given by directors in interviews.

[a]Founded in early 1971; data is for July, 1971.

Ignacio Guevara left the Interamerican church in the center of Bogota, where he had been the pastor. Guevara had become convinced of Pentecostal doctrine and determined to start an independent church in the capital city. Church services were begun in a home in 1956, and almost half of the people from the Interamerican church that Guevara had pastored followed him in this new church, which later took the name Panamerican Mission.[12] This division seems to have come as a result of genuine conviction on Guevara's part, but it did strike a blow to the Interamerican work there.

This new and completely indigenous church grew in just as exceptional a way in Bogota as did the Assemblies of God. In fact, in 1967, the Panamerican churches had more members in the capital than the Assemblies of God did, and likely would be just as large as the Assemblies today if it were not for the division which took place in their churches in Bogota in 1968.

At that time, the pastor of the second largest Panamerican church in Bogota was accused of living in immorality. When

confronted with this by Guevara and other Panamerican
leaders, the pastor in question accused Guevara of being a dictator and influenced his own church, and others, to form a
new church, called Members of the Body of Christ.[13] Half of
the Panamerican churches and members in Bogota were lost
to this newly formed group. Today the Members of the Body
of Christ church claims more members in Bogota than does
the Panamerican Mission.

In the annual convention of the United Pentecostal Church,
in 1967, the Colombian church leaders and delegates voted to
nationalize their church, with Colombians taking over the
complete administration of the churches. The missionaries
from the United States did not accept this, and resigned from
the newly formed Colombian United Pentecostal Church.[14]

One of the places most affected by this division was Bogota,
where the Thompsons, missionaries who are particularly strong
leaders, are located. Several churches in Bogota were divided
over whether to stay with the Colombian church, or to split
from it with the missionaries. As a result, one of the churches
in Bogota, several Colombian leaders, and a number of members from other churches, withdrew with the missionaries to
work with them. The split set the Colombian United Pentecostal Church back somewhat in Bogota, and if it had not
been for this division, it would likely be the largest in membership in this city today. But the split does not seem to have hurt
the growth rate of either of the groups; both have been experiencing good growth since the division.

Even the small Church of God has had a split, though it
did not affect their membership significantly. This church is
affiliated with the Pentecostal denomination of the same name
in the United States, with headquarters in Cleveland, Ten-
nessee. Ricardo Moreno began this work in Bogota in 1961,
and in 1963 their first church was organized. By 1970, there
were three small churches in Bogota with a total membership
of about 95. Then, when Ricardo became unsatisfied with one
of his pastor's efforts, the pastor in question separated from the
Church of God to form a new church called the Church of God

of Prophecy.[15] This church is now affiliated with the denomination of the same name in the United States, which in turn is an offshoot of the Church of God, and which came out of the Church of God amid a great deal of scandal and lawsuits in the 1920s.[16] The Church of God of Prophecy now claims one small church in Bogota, with about fifty members and two preaching points.[17]

PEREIRA

The oldest Protestant church in Pereira is the Cumberland Presbyterian. This work was originally founded by Brethren missionaries in 1940, but later was turned over to the Presbyterians, who constructed a lovely church building on the present site in 1949.

The Cumberland Presbyterian Mission began its work in Colombia in 1927 in the city of Cali. Evangelistic services were begun in that same year in a large house, and in 1928, the Colegio Americano was founded in this city. Their first church was organized in 1929, and from there the work spread to other cities in the Valle and Caldas regions.[18]

The Presbyterian church of Pereira is one of Cumberland's older and larger churches. In 1969, its membership was 135, with an average attendance of 170. This church, however, has had very little growth in recent years: the average attendance of 163 in 1960 increased to only 170 in 1969. Membership growth has been modest, increasing from 87 to 135 in the same period, and most of this increase took place from 1960 to 1966. From 1967 to 1969 there has been no real increase in membership.

The United Pentecostals and Southern Baptists were the next to initiate efforts in Pereira in the years 1956 and 1957, respectively. The Baptists began well, and experienced fair growth up until 1963, when attendance reached 135 and membership fifty-two. Then a period of declension set in, and by 1969, attendance had dropped to half its former level, and membership to thirty-five. Since then, both membership and attendance have again been on the rise. Two changes took place in 1969: (1) the Baptist church ceased to rent houses for meetings, and initiated services in a beautiful new church building with a very good location; and (2) an active student pastor took charge of the work. By early 1970 attendance was a little over one hundred.

The United Pentecostal Church has had by far the greatest growth in Pereira. It was founded in 1956, and by 1960, there were 50 members, and approximately 100 in attendance in the house where they were meeting. By 1966, the central church had 450 members, and in 1967 the second church was founded in a very populated *barrio* on the outskirts of the city; 50 members from the central church formed the nucleus for the starting of the new church. By 1969 the central church had grown to 550 members, and the second church to 310, for a combined total membership of 860 members.

The Jesus Only churches here have also been very active in reaching out to surrounding areas. When I interviewed the pastor of the second church, Abelardo Galvis, in February of 1969, this church had thirteen preaching points in neighboring towns and settlements. By September of that same year—seven months later—the number had increased to twenty-one. The central church had five preaching points at that time, making a total of twenty-six regular preaching points. These efforts prompted the Presbyterian pastor to answer, when I asked him where the Pentecostals were working in the area: "Don't ask where the Pentecostals are working; ask where they are *not* working. We see them everywhere we go, going to hold services in different places."[19]

The Panamerican Mission founded its work in Pereira in 1960. Segundo Tellez, a leading layman from the Panamerican church in Bogota, came with his family and began meetings in a home with a handful of people. The church has had almost steady progress since then, and although this progress is modest compared to that of the United Pentecostals, the Panamerican church has had the best growth rate of the Trinitarian Protestant churches in Pereira. By 1969, the original membership of 3 in 1960, had grown to 102, and attendance from 7 to 150.

One of the exceptional things about this church is that it had founded, by 1969, three incipient churches in other towns in the region—Pueblo Rico, Salamina, and El Cairo. Laymen from the Pereira church have founded, and are now directing, these congregations. And besides these three towns, the Panamerican church in Pereira had three regular preaching points in *barrios* of the city.

The GMU founded its work in Pereira as most churches have done, by beginning with a few interested people, then visiting, teaching, and preaching until there were converts, baptisms, and the organization of a local church. Meetings were begun in 1965 in a rented house, also used as a bookstore-reading room. The work prospered under missionary leadership, and after eighteen months, there were twenty-eight members and an average attendance of seventy-five. In mid-1966, a national pastor took the direction of the church, and unfortunately, the membership declined to thirteen and attendance to forty-two by early 1968. As to the reasons for these losses, GMU leaders list these: (1) an overdependence on the missionaries that had started the church, as so often happens in these cases; (2) a professional attitude on the part of the national pastor toward the ministry that expressed itself in an attitude of "Since I'm the trained pastor here, I run the show"; (this stifled the leadership within the church and brought strained relations between the pastor and these leaders); (3) there were personality problems between the senior missionary that remained and the incoming pastor.[20]

Since 1968 there has been a rebuilding, and the GMU church has recovered its previous losses, so that by the end of 1969, membership and attendance were back to their previous levels. Under the present national pastor, the Pereira church has opened a branch work in the city's most populous suburb, and is in charge of a new work in the neighboring city of Cartago.

It has already been mentioned that of the non-Pentecostal

denominations included in this study, the Christian and Missionary Alliance has had one of the best growth rates in recent years. The CMA work in Colombia was initiated in 1925, first in the Cali area, then in Popayan. Clyde Taylor founded the Alliance Bible Institute in the city of Armenia, in the Caldas region, in the early thirties, and directed evangelistic efforts in this area. The first CMA church in Armenia was organized in 1933, and in 1934, work was initiated in the city of Manizales, resulting in the establishment of another church there.[21]

Although Armenia is only about thirty miles from Pereira, and has been a center for the CMA since the thirties, efforts to found a church in Pereira did not really begin until 1966, a short time after the GMU began its work there. There were a few Christians in Pereira affiliated with the CMA, so the pastor and a lay leader from the Manizales church began to visit these believers and hold services with them. In 1966 the lay leader from Manizales moved to Pereira to pastor this new church. Part of a building was rented for services, and a bookstore-reading room was opened downtown, under the direction of CMA missionaries. Since then the growth of the church has been modest but steady, and by 1969 the initial membership of two has increased to thirty, and attendance to sixty-eight.[22]

The Assemblies of God entered Pereira last, in 1968, but founded their church in a different way than the others. Unlike the previous denominations, which began their churches by meeting with a small handful of interested people, and then building up a church by visitation, Bible study, and preaching, the Assemblies of God began their church in Pereira with an extended evangelistic campaign. Held in a vacant lot in Pereira in March of 1968, the "Campaign of Faith in Christ and Divine Healing" was organized by Everett Divine, Assemblies of God missionary who had moved to Cali in 1967. An Assemblies pastor from the United States gave the messages with the use of an interpreter. A Colombian layman from the Assemblies church in Cali also formed part of the campaign team. Each evening, decisions were made, and during the day

these people were visited by the Assemblies of God team. By
the end of the special campaign, a lot had been purchased near
the campaign site, and a simple meeting place had been constructed. The converts and interested people from the campaign were simply channeled into the new church building as
soon as the special meetings ended.[23]

Attendance in the new site was between one hundred and
two hundred in the beginning, and sixty converts entered the
first baptismal class. In June, the first thirty were baptized,
and the lay leader from the Cali church became the pastor of
the new congregation. A very rapid and promising beginning
had been made; but this new work, which in a very short time
had bought a property, built a simple structure, baptized thirty,
and organized as a church, fell into hard times with its largely
unproven pastor. There soon were problems of poor testimony,
instability, and dissatisfaction, and the church suffered as a
result. From a membership of over thirty and attendance of
over one hundred at the beginning, the membership fell to
twenty-two and attendance to forty-five by the fall of 1969.

But this does not mean that the extended-campaign method
of planting churches has not worked for the Assemblies of God.
In a period of four years, under the leadership of Everett Divine, this method has been used to establish a number of new
congregations in the Valle, Caldas, and Cauca regions.

The total picture in Pereira shows only three churches of any
size in 1969—the Pentecostal, Presbyterian, and Panamerican,
though the Baptist church is picking up again. Of the churches
just mentioned, one—the Presbyterian—has the longest history
in Pereira, but has grown very little in recent years. Three of
the Pereira churches—the Southern Baptist, GMU, and Assemblies of God—have suffered serious setbacks at some time
since they were founded. And though all of them have recovered, or are recovering their losses, these setbacks have
affected adversely the growth picture for these churches.
Pereira has been a difficult city for most denominations working there.

The *only* church which has experienced really exceptional

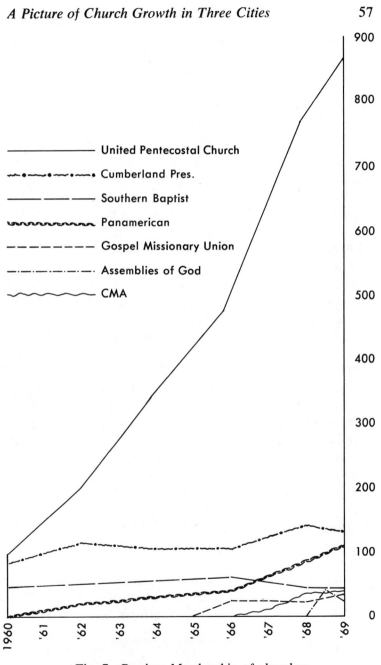

Fig. 7. Pereira: Membership of churches

church growth is the United Pentecostal. None of the other churches have come close to their growth, though the Panamerican has had respectable growth in comparison to the others.

PALMIRA

The Gospel Missionary Union was the first Protestant mission to enter the western part of Colombia, in 1908. Early efforts were aimed at introducing the Bible and its message in as many towns and cities as possible in western Colombia. This was done through colportage efforts, Bible sales on market days, and meetings in the homes of interested people in the different communities visited. Cali became the center for GMU activities, and the first believers were baptized there in 1921.[24]

From Cali, the GMU work spread to Palmira, about twenty miles away, where GMU missionaries founded the first Protestant church in this city in the early twenties. Along with the evangelistic and church-planting efforts here, the GMU established a Bible institute in 1924, Maranatha Hospital in 1944, and later a Christian day school and an evangelical bookstore.[25] The Bible institute was closed in 1968, after forty years of existence, because of the decreasing student body, and the conviction, especially on the part of the missionaries, that the institute was not accomplishing the purpose for which it was founded: to train leaders that would plant and build growing churches.* The GMU is now using the seminary extension program, and residence students attend the CMA Bible institute in Armenia, or the Southern Baptist seminary in Cali.

The second GMU church in Palmira was organized in 1957, and the third in 1958, so that there were churches in three different sectors of the city. Most of the believers that formed the nucleus to begin these two churches were members of the central church, reducing that church's membership. The hope was that the three churches would prosper and experience far

---

*In fact, according to William Shillingsburg, veteran GMU missionary, the time when the GMU church growth in Colombia began to slow down was when a full Bible institute program was introduced. A professional attitude that had not existed before toward the ministry entered the churches.

more church growth than the central church alone could achieve. For a while, things did begin to work this way: in the first years, all three churches experienced growth. Before the second and third churches were founded, the central church had grown to a membership of 125, and attendance to 260. By 1966, when the GMU hit its peak in Palmira, the total membership of the three churches was a little over 200, and attendance 420. Since then, however, there has been a decline in all three churches, and by 1970 the total membership had dropped to 132, and attendance to 275, almost the same level at which they had been in the central church alone in the mid-fifties.

Several of the reasons that are apparent in this decline are: (1) the churches became accustomed to capable, experienced, and well-trained pastors and missionaries in the first years; later, when less gifted and trained pastors had to take over, the churches suffered; (2) Palmira was a seedbed of problems and dissensions within the GMU in the later sixties, and though this has largely been overcome, it did affect the churches; (3) there has been a rapid turnover of pastors in these churches; (4) a growing indifference has been observed in the Palmira churches, with a corresponding loss of interest in soul-winning and outreach. There does, however, seem to be an awakening in two of the churches at present, with an accompanying upward growth trend.

The next denominations to found churches in Palmira were the Southern Baptist and United Pentecostal, in 1954. Since then, the Southern Baptist church has experienced fairly constant, though modest, church growth. With an increase of membership from 18 in 1954, to 75 in 1961, and 150 in 1971, the Baptist church has the best overall growth rate of the non-Pentecostal churches in Palmira.

The United Pentecostal Church, however, has had a rapid and impressive rate of growth. Membership increased from 20 in 1954, to 250 in 1960, and by 1970 to 1,020! The next closest Protestant church in membership in 1970 was the Baptist, with 136—quite a difference.

The United Pentecostal Church really had its beginnings in Colombia when the Verner Larsens came as the first missionaries of the unitarian Pentecostal faith, in 1936. They were sponsored at that time by the Pentecostal Assembly of Jesus Christ, based in Canada. In 1938, the Larsens established the first unitarian Pentecostal church in Colombia in the city of Bucaramanga, and in the early forties, the second church in Barranquilla, on the Atlantic coast.[26]

In 1945, the Pentecostal Assemblies of Jesus Christ and the United Pentecostal Church, Inc., united to form the United Pentecostal Church.[27] This newly formed body sent three new missionaries to Colombia in 1949. At that time, there were just the two churches in Bucaramanga and Barranquilla, but no Pentecostals of any kind in the department of the Valle, or the neighboring regions.

Two of the newly sent missionaries were Mr. and Mrs. William Drost, who arrived in Cali, the major city of the Valle, in 1949. Meetings were begun in the Drost home, and soon after, in other points in the surrounding area. Within a year, several congregations had been founded and over five hundred converts were baptized! By 1959, just ten years after the first Pentecostal missionaries arrived in Cali, there were over twenty organized churches and preaching points in the departments of the Valle and Caldas.[28] Sally Morley, who had come to Colombia as a single missionary in 1948, described the beginnings of the Pentecostal work in this region:

> A man named Johnston had come to Cali with the Pentecostal church, and although he didn't start a church, he began prayer meetings. The William Drost family came to Cali in 1949, and later I came to work with them, in 1951. The Drosts had begun a church in their own home in Cali when I came, and the work had spread to the mountains. Drost was very evangelistic and got out a lot; his converts did the same thing. Some that had come from other areas to live in Cali, went back to their home areas, evangelized, then invited Drost and others to visit. Groups that formed in this way were later organized as churches, with lay leaders becoming the pastors of these churches.[29]

Drost himself was really what might be termed a "lay missionary." He had received no formal theological education and understood little about the proper procedure of missionaries in beginning a new work. Very soon after people were converted, he would send them out to evangelize in the surrounding areas, not realizing that it was not "orthodox" to send untrained and inexperienced believers to preach as though they were trained pastors. This was something that had not been done by the other Pentecostal missionaries up to this time, and some of them did not agree with this way of doing things. But it was in this area where the Drosts were working that the United Pentecostal Church really began to grow and expand at a rapid pace.[30]

The first Pentecostal efforts in Palmira began with the visits of believers from their church in Cali. In 1953, cottage meetings were started with a group of about twenty. By 1959, the attendance had grown to over 150, and the construction of a large temple was begun. The new building was designed to serve not only as a meeting place for the local believers, but also as a convention center for this part of Colombia. In the following years, thousands of zealous Jesus Only people from the neighboring regions would gather here for their mass rallies and conferences.[31]

In 1962, with 350 members in the central church, the Pentecostals decided to organize the second church in an outlying *barrio* called La Emilia. By 1970, this church grew from 20 to 270 members: the membership of the smaller second church alone had surpassed that of any other denomination in Palmira.[32]

The Cumberland Presbyterians followed the Southern Baptists and the Pentecostals in establishing a work in Palmira, founding a church there in 1959. But their growth has been very slow, and the small congregation still meets in an old house with limited facilities. Membership increased from twelve in 1959 to forty-four in 1966, but in the next five years showed an increase of only three, to a total of forty-seven members in 1971. Attendance actually decreased slightly, from an average of fifty in 1966, to forty-five in 1971.[33]

The Assemblies of God founded the latest Protestant church in Palmira, in 1967. Some of the Assemblies believers from Cali began to visit Palmira in 1966, and by early 1967 there was a small group meeting there. The same method was then used as had been used in Pereira; an extended evangelistic campaign was held in a vacant lot in one of Palmira's popular *barrios*. Those who made decisions during the campaign were visited and encouraged, and some were later enrolled in baptismal classes. A modest meeting place was erected on the vacant lot which had been the site of the campaign. The church got its start with fifteen members and an average attendance of approximately sixty.

The Assemblies of God church is still small, but has at least had constant growth since its beginning, having avoided the problems that plagued the Pereira church. Membership increased from fifteen in 1967 to thirty-four in 1971, and attendance from sixty to seventy-five. About a third of the members had belonged to other evangelical churches in the city.[34]

This, then, gives a general description of church growth in Palmira. The GMU, which is the oldest established mission, hit its peak in 1966, but since then has suffered losses in membership in all three of its churches. The Presbyterian church, after more than ten years, is still very small and is not growing. Of the non-Pentecostal churches, only the Southern Baptist has experienced fair growth up to the present. The Assemblies of God is the newest church in Palmira, and though small, is growing. But it is again the United Pentecostal Church which, in comparison to the others, has had very rapid and exceptional growth, with seven times as many members in 1971, as the next largest Protestant denomination here.

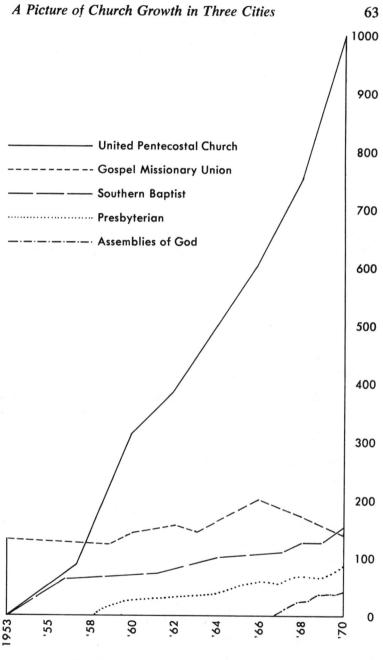

Fig. 8. Palmira: Membership of churches

4

Pentecostal Distinctives

Who are the Pentecostals, and what do they believe? What guiding beliefs, standards, and characteristics do they have in common? Certainly there are some differences between the Pentecostal denominations in Colombia. The Jesus Only people hold to certain doctrines which are unique to them, are very exclusive toward other Protestant churches, and are more emotional and extreme in their church services and the charismatic manifestations, than are the rest of the Pentecostal denominations. Yet despite these differences, the various Pentecostal churches share certain basic distinctives. John Nichol writes,

> These events which occurred on the Day of Pentecost constitute the very core of modern Pentecostal belief and practice. Whatever else may separate them, all Pentecostals agree that like the 120 who had gathered in the upper room, they too must "tarry" and "be endued with power from on high." They take seriously and personally the Petrine challenge to the gathered multitude on the Day of Pentecost: "Repent and be baptized every one of you in the name of Jesus Christ for the remission of your sins, and you shall receive the gift of the Holy Spirit. For the promise is to you and to your children" [Ac 2:28-39]. Very simply, then, the now nearly 8 million Pentecostals bear that name because they are convinced of "the reality of a present-day experience for . . . believers such as was received by the early disciples on the Day of Pentecost" [Earl P. Paulk, Jr., *Your Pentecostal Neighbor* (Cleveland, Tenn.: Pathway, 1958), p. 61].[1]

EMPHASIS ON THE CHARISMATIC GIFTS
OF THE HOLY SPIRIT

Without a doubt, the major distinctive of the Pentecostals is belief in, and emphasis upon, the Holy Spirit and the charismatic gifts that He imparts. Nichol says,

> Despite the rather close similarity in so many areas, the great gulf which separates most Protestants from the Pentecostals is the stress which the latter put on what they call the "full gospel"—especially the teaching concerning one's experiential encounter with the Holy Spirit, as well as the emphasis on healing.[2]

Ignacio Vergara, a Chilean Roman Catholic priest, writes that the Pentecostals

> sustain that the communication of the Holy Spirit promised by Jesus (Jn. 16:7; Acts 1:8) and realized in the apostles and disciples on the day of Pentecost (Acts 2:1-11) was not a single and isolated event, that happened but once in the history of the Church, but rather continues to take place in all periods of the Church. The Holy Spirit continues to communicate Himself to the believers in the same way and with the same extraordinary manifestations, as on the day of Pentecost and on subsequent occasions (Acts 10:44-46; 19:6).[3]

Prudencio Damboriena adds,

> These groups called themselves "Pentecostal" because they believed that upon them had fallen the effusion of the graces of a new Pentecost, accompanied by the charismatic gifts (of tongues, prophecy, and healing) of the first apostles.[4]

What are these charismatic gifts and manifestations that the Pentecostals expect the Holy Spirit to impart to them?

BAPTISM OF THE SPIRIT

Also referred to as "the promise of the Father" and the "baptism of fire," the baptism of the Holy Spirit is an experience, subsequent to conversion, in which the Spirit comes upon the believer, empowering the person to live and witness victoriously, and imparting spiritual gifts (such as tongues, prophecy, healing) by which the believer can perform the supernatural.

> To all believers has been given this right, so that they ought to ardently wait for and seek with earnestness the Promise of the Father: the baptism in the Holy Spirit and in fire, according to the commandment of our Lord. This was the normal experience of all the believers in the early Church. As a result of this experience, comes the giving of power from on high for living, service, and the dispensation of the gifts to be used in the work of the ministry. . . . This marvellous experience is distinct and subsequent to that of the new birth.[5]

The new believer is encouraged to seek this experience by waiting before the Lord in a spirit of expectancy; he is to empty himself of all other thoughts and to concentrate on the Holy Spirit. When the "baptism" comes, it is usually a pleasurable or highly emotional experience whereby the recipient "feels good all over," has "visions of heavenly beauty," hears the Lord and angels speaking to him, or as was expressed in a number of interviews, "feels waves of what seem like electrical currents" flowing through the body. One Pentecostal believer described his experience this way:

> We were in a meeting at the church. After the message the pastor said: "Those who want to receive the baptism of the Holy Spirit come forward, and those of us that have already received it are going to help you." I went forward, kneeled, and lifted my hands, praying for the baptism. Then I entered in contact with God; I felt joy in my body; I felt as though I were being lifted in the air. Then my tongue was loosed and I began to speak in tongues.[6]

Each experience is somewhat different, but there is a pattern that runs through the testimonies. Usually there is an after-meeting, in which new believers are encouraged to seek "the Promise." The older believers gather around the ones seeking the baptism, and all begin to pray. The tempo increases until the seekers are almost beside themselves; then all of a sudden, one or more of the new believers erupts, speaking in unintelligible phrases. This is the climax; the seeker has "prayed through" with the help of the brethren, and has received the sign of the baptism of the Holy Spirit. All praise God for this fresh outpouring of His Spirit upon His children.

GLOSSALALIA

For Pentecostals, the initial sign of having received the baptism of the Holy Spirit is speaking in tongues. The *Reglamento* of the Assemblies of God, which is their basic manual for new believers, states: "The baptism of the Holy Spirit identifies itself by the initial sign of speaking in an unknown tongue under the Spirit's influence."[7] Every Pentecostal believer should have this initial experience.

Some Pentecostal churches, such as the Assemblies of God, distinguish between speaking in tongues as a *sign* of the baptism of the Holy Spirit, and tongues as a *gift* imparted to some believers for their own and the church's edification. In this sense, it is an experience whereby the Spirit comes upon a believer with the gift, enabling this Christian to speak in special languages (often called "angelic" or "heavenly" languages), and through which the Spirit may convey a message to the congregation. When the person speaking in tongues goes into a trance-like state in a meeting, another, called an interpreter, may translate the message to the congregation. These messages are believed to come from God.

Denominations such as the Panamerican Mission and the Assemblies of God, stress interpretation of tongues more than the United Pentecostal Church, where there is little attempt at control. But this also varies between churches within the same denomination. In one meeting of an Assemblies of God church, I heard six women speak in tongues at different times during the service (no men spoke in tongues in that service), but there was no interpretation at any of these occasions.

Speaking in tongues is usually a highly emotional experience. A member of the Panamerican church in Pereira described his initial experience:

One time I was praying in a meeting. I believed very little in this matter of tongues, and had doubts. But on May 20, 1967, in a prayer meeting in church, as I was praying in a very concentrated way, all of a sudden I felt as if someone had turned a very strong searchlight on me and I was burning. I was going to speak in Spanish, but couldn't. I couldn't see anything but flames of fire all around me, and I felt as if I were burning. Then I began to speak in tongues. I was conscious, but I was in ecstasy.[8]

Another, a Jesus Only Pentecostal, said:

After my conversion, I was in a meeting, and after the service I went forward to kneel and pray. There were many others praying also, to help me. I began to speak in tongues and felt a joy and happiness that I had never felt before. I felt joy in all my body. Since then I have spoken in tongues many times and in many services.[9]

Another believer added, "It can happen anywhere, but one has to concentrate completely on the Lord, and humble oneself before the presence of the Lord."[10]

DIVINE HEALING

From the beginning of the Pentecostal movement, the doctrine of divine healing has been one of its cardinal tenets. Healing has been preached and practiced because Pentecostals believe that "deliverance from physical sickness is provided for in the atonement of Jesus Christ and is the privilege of all believers."[11] They also emphasize the text in Exodus 15:26 where the Lord declares, "I am the LORD that healeth thee," and the fact that healing was such an important part of Christ's ministry while on earth. Pentecostals also point out that the gift of healing is mentioned by the apostle Paul in 1 Corinthians 12:9, and that healing is one of the supernatural signs that Christ promised would follow those that believe: "And these signs shall follow them that believe . . . they shall lay hands on the sick, and they shall recover" (Mk 16:17a, 18b).

Pentecostals believe that healing can be received in several ways. One of the more obvious is in response to the invitation to healing given in evangelistic and healing campaigns, or after a regular meeting in a local church.

Another means of healing is for the sick believer to call the elders of the church, who will come, pray for him, and encourage him to get right with the Lord if there is something in his life that might be bringing the chastisement of sickness. This promise, of course, is for the whole believing church, but the Pentecostals practice it much more than other Protestants.

The third means of healing is for the sick believer simply to exercise faith in the power of Christ to heal, and to ask for healing in the name of Jesus Christ. A doctrinal booklet of the United Pentecostal Church states:

> Divine healing is one of the signs that follow those that believe, not just to some individuals, but to all believers. God uses different members of the Church . . . giving gifts of healing, working miracles, etc. . . . It is the privilege of every believer that is ill to call the elders of the church, so that they can pray for him, and anoint him with oil, and the prayer of faith will heal the sick (James 5:14-16). We do not believe that man can heal the sick of himself, but that the power of God working in the Body of Christ heals through the instrumentality of those members that are gifted for this ministry. . . . Healing can also come as a result of the prayer of the just man that believes with all faith.[12]

The sickness or physical problem for which healing is sought may vary from blindness or lameness, to a headache or a sore foot. But there are very few Pentecostals that cannot point to some time and experience when they sought or prayed for healing, and are convinced that they received it from the Lord. In one interview with a Panamerican church member, this experience of healing was related to me:

> I had acute sinusitis. In a prayer meeting, a brother received the gift of tongues and said that "a sick person that is here should come forward." I went forward, sure that God had healed me. . . . At another time I had amoebas that were causing me the beginnings of an ulcer. The brethren prayed for me, and I was healed.[13]

Another, a member of a United Pentecostal church, gave this story of his experience of healing on one occasion:

> I was sick with a tremendous fever. At noon I came home from the market and lay down. At two o'clock a brother came from the church and prayed for me. I got worse, and the devil was working tremendously. At four o'clock in the afternoon, other brethren came; I was worse now. One believer said, "Brother, you are going to believe with all your heart that you are going to be healed." They began to pray, and one brother spoke in tongues. I felt a current run through my body, and then I felt cold all over. The brethren told me to sit up and said, "Now you are healed." That night I went to the church meeting, completely healed.[14]

The opinions of Pentecostals vary regarding the use of medicines and doctors. One says, "I haven't used drugs and don't believe I'll have to use them. It is a lack of faith to use medicines."[15] Another differs with this, and says, "I think it is all right for a believer to go to a doctor, if one doesn't have sufficient faith. As far as medicines, I think it's all right to take little things like Alka-Seltzer, aspirin, vitamins, and so on."[16] Until recently, it was a grave sin of disbelief for a Jesus Only member to go to a doctor or use medicines. This position has moderated somewhat in some of their churches, and even some of the pastors now use drugs for sickness on occasion. But much fanaticism still exists in this regard in the United Pentecostal Church, and some of the results are very sad. The GMU administers the evangelical cemetery in Palmira, and those who keep track of burials say there is a disproportionately high number of deaths among the Jesus Only people. Even babies and children that have nothing more serious than parasites or diarrhea are often allowed to die, because the parents consider it a sin to seek medical help. Yet from my interviews with different Pentecostal pastors and leaders, it is clear that there are some that have a more practical and moderate way of looking at these things, and want to avoid extremes of fanaticism in matters such as healing.

We do not condemn the believer that seeks medical help when he feels that his faith is not sufficient for the miracle of healing. The main thing is to place one's trust in God in every case of sickness.[17]

PROPHECY

"As speaking in tongues is supernatural utterance in an unknown tongue, so prophecy is a supernatural utterance in a known tongue. It is a manifestation of the Spirit of God, and not of the human mind."[18]

Here the Holy Spirit is said to illuminate the believer with the gift of prophecy, enabling this Christian to understand some truth in a special way, or to prophesy concerning a future event. I found more emphasis on the use of prophecy in this way in the Panamerican churches than in the other Pentecostal churches under study.

Related to the gift of prophecy are the gifts of wisdom and knowledge. According to a study manual put out by the Panamerican Mission, the gift of wisdom is "a supernatural gift of revelation and the wisdom of God, given by the Holy Spirit. It brings a word of wisdom from God of His plans and purposes for an individual or a group." The gift of the word of knowledge is defined in a similar way, being "a supernatural gift of revelation and knowledge given by the Holy Spirit, that brings a word of knowledge of God concerning any act or matter."[19]

While certain Christians are believed to have the gift of prophecy, or the related gifts just mentioned, others that do not have these gifts may have the experience of receiving special light and understanding on some truth, future event, or a matter regarding a brother or the local church, through a dream or vision. Many of the Pentecostal members interviewed had at some time had this kind of experience, and while most of the dreams seemed to be the normal working of the subconscious, to the persons interviewed, they had special divine meaning and often had been a special blessing. A United Pentecostal man explained how a dream had encouraged him as a new believer:

> When I was very recently converted, I saw a form of net
> that came down from heaven. The angel told me to get in.
> Then they swung me back and forth and I heard celestial
> music and voices. This gave me much encouragement.[20]

A woman from the Panamerican church in Pereira described
what she feels was a vision:

> I had a vision with my own eyes. I was praying by the bed,
> and it was very dark in the room. When I opened my eyes,
> I saw a bright light behind the bed, like a mercury light. I
> said, "Could it be the Holy Spirit?" My husband didn't see
> it and said, "It must be a firefly." I did not see anything
> except the light, but I know that it was the Holy Spirit.[21]

Many of the dreams and visions have to do with the second
coming of Christ, heaven, or with Christ's calling people to
Himself. When I asked one believer from the Panamerican
church whether he had ever had a dream or vision, he replied:

> The majority of those baptized in the Spirit have had them.
> When I was recently converted, I had a dream in which I
> saw the depths of hell itself. There was a very large open
> oven made of what looked like lava, boiling with melted lead,
> and filled with thousands of souls that made the worst cries.
> There was also a gangplank from which the souls were falling.
> I was in the center of all this but did not suffer anything.
> After this, I saw a blue heaven above, and a very narrow path-
> way like a red ribbon, and beyond this the most beautiful
> heaven and a door. I saw the crucified Christ at the door.[22]

PERSUASION

Pentecostals strongly believe that the Holy Spirit transforms
every consecrated believer into a zealous and convincing evangelist and witness, who finds himself under an irresistible com-
pulsion to spread the good news of the gospel. Speaking of the
Pentecostal contribution, McGavran writes:

> Just as the Holy Spirit causes believers to speak in an
> unpredictable fashion, so He will also lead them to do what
> "seems good to the Holy Spirit." . . . He will send Christians

> to preach. He will give them power to persuade. He will
> heal at their hands, and give heed to their prayer. . . . They
> are free to do what in their circumstances seems good to them.
> . . . The principle of *spontaneous action under the control of
> the Spirit of Jesus as revealed in the Scriptures* lies at the heart
> of the Pentecostal faith. Anything which the situation re-
> quires is permissible—provided the Holy Spirit . . . ap-
> proves.[23]

The Pentecostal is made to understand that he does not have
to have special theological education nor be a Christian for
many years to be an effective soul-winner, or to see the power
of God working through his life. It is enough to know Christ
as Saviour, and to have received the baptism and filling of the
Holy Spirit. This conviction was expressed very clearly in a
sermon preached by Jesus Cardozo, pastor of the First United
Pentecostal Church in Palmira; his text was from 1 Corinthians
12:

> God is still a God of miracles. He is the same yesterday,
> today, and forever. First Corinthians 12:10 is not speaking
> of the great works of exceptional men, but of the supernatural
> works of God through men. One of the greatest miracles is
> the conversion of men to Christ. But God also says that
> there will be supernatural signs and works done in the name
> of His holy Son. Glory to God! . . . We think that maybe a
> man with much study, much capacity, much strength can do
> miracles and great things. But no! Any man, any woman,
> any person can do miracles with the power of the Holy Spirit.
> Glory to God! . . . The greatest gift of miracles is to deliver
> from spiritual death; to raise lost souls from the spiritual
> dead. . . . We want to speak to souls; we want to win others.
> We can't go on this way; the world must see something in
> us, must see the power of the Holy Spirit working through us.
> We want to win them. We want to see the power of God
> working in souls. Amen![24]

In resumé, three things are of utmost importance to Pentecostals: (1) the charismatic gifts and manifestations; (2) subjective experience; and (3) personal and aggressive witness for
Christ, corroborated by supernatural signs. For a Pentecostal

to live without experiencing the "baptism of fire," speaking in tongues, divine healing, and special visions or dreams, would be to take the heart out of his Christian life and experience. These are the distinctives that make him a Pentecostal.

One of the questions on the interviews with Pentecostal members was, Which beliefs are most important to you? Of twenty-four individual members interviewed, twenty-three mentioned the baptism of the Holy Spirit, while conversion was mentioned eighteen times. Perhaps some that did not mention conversion took this for granted, but it is still significant that more of them included the baptism of the Holy Spirit than conversion. Healing followed the Holy Spirit baptism and conversion in importance to those interviewed, being mentioned nine times. Other beliefs included less often were baptism in the name of Christ, the second coming, tongues, holiness, prophecy, and the working of miracles, in that order.

Personal subjective experience and feeling was emphasized frequently in the interviews with Pentecostal members. The question was asked, Do you have assurance that you are saved? Following this was the question, How do you know? I wanted to find out if the majority interviewed would base their assurance on the Word of God, or on subjective feeling and experience. The latter won out: while some did mention the work of Christ and the promises of the Bible, especially among the Trinitarian Pentecostals interviewed, the majority based their assurance on feelings. These were some of the replies from Pentecostal church members to the question, How do you know you are saved? (Italics below are mine).

"Because I *feel* the presence of God like an electrical current. When I *feel* empty and far from God I kneel and cry to God. Then I again *feel* that I have salvation."

"Because of the peace and love that I *feel* toward God. It is a supernatural thing. Sometimes this peace is lost and one *feels* cold spiritually. Then when one seeks God, one is again satisfied."

"I *feel* salvation as one *feels* the wind. I *feel* it inside. Since my conversion I have *felt* rest and pardon."

"Because I have experienced it in my life. Salvation is something that is *felt*."

"Each one *feels* how he ought to walk before God, and whether he is right with God. I *feel* assurance of my salvation."

"Because I *feel* salvation through the Holy Spirit. While the Holy Spirit is within a person, there is salvation."

INTENSE EMOTIONAL CHARACTER OF ITS MEETINGS

The Roman Catholic priest, Damboriena, referring to Latin American Pentecostals in general, describes their services in this way:

> Their services distinguish themselves by several characteristics. The first of these refers to the vitality of their meetings. . . . The liturgy is simple, carried forward on the basis of emotionalism in which common manifestations are trances, speaking in tongues, and special inspirations of all kinds. . . . The Pentecostals attribute a great deal of importance to their meetings, which have as their object, not so much the worship of God, as religious instruction, the mutual fellowship of the faithful, and the contagious emotionalism . . . that is reached in the services.[25]

Vergara refers to this contagious emotionalism as "collective psychosis,"[26] and John Considine's description of their meetings seem to fit this description:

> Its religious meetings are classical expressions of highly emotional gatherings at which the preacher with agitated shouts stirs his flock and the flock reacts with continued interruptions of "Aleluia! Amen! Praise be to God!" As the tempo mounts individuals feel inspired, fall to the floor in trances, are called on by the preacher to reveal to the brethren what they have received from the Spirit. If the preacher has done his job well, every member of the flock goes home thrilled by the wonderful experience.[27]

The United Pentecostal Church is the most extreme in the emotional character of its meetings. I visited the second United Pentecostal Church in Pereira on a Saturday night. The building, a temporary one of bamboo-slat walls and palm sections for floors, was full of people; there were between three hundred and four hundred in attendance. As the meeting got under way, everyone was very happy and exuberant. On the platform, an enthusiastic and capable young man led the singing to the accompaniment of guitars and maracas (dried gourds filled with seeds). Some of the people were standing, and almost all were clapping and singing; it was a real fiesta of exuberance and noise. The leader then asked, "How many will give testimony to the glory of God?" No coaxing was needed. One believer after another stood to speak of what God had done for him or her personally, and the congregation interjected with "Amen! Glory to God! Hallelujah!" Then the pastor led in prayer. It was a loud experience with everyone praying at once. The praying of the people soon drowned out the pastor, and was something like the dull roar of an advancing train that grew until it hit a climax of sound and intensity. Some were standing, others kneeling; almost all were lifting and waving their arms toward heaven, and, with grimaced faces and lips, were pleading for God's blessing and power to be manifested. Then, as though on cue, the roar subsided until there was again relative quietness. Many non-Pentecostals were watching from the outside, and I felt that many of them, as myself, did not feel at home in this charged-up atmosphere. But there is no doubt that it attracts the attention of the people who come to see what it is all about, and by their growth it is obvious that it appeals to many.

Some of the Pentecostal denominations—especially the Assemblies of God and Panamerican Mission—are characterized by a more moderate form of emotionalism in their meetings, and within these denominations, the type of meeting generally follows the convictions and taste of the local pastor and leaders.

There seems to exist a tendency for emotional extremes in Pentecostal meetings to diminish with the passing of time and as leaders gain more education and experience.

Sociologists of religion claim that when sects such as the Pentecostals first emerge they tend toward religious extremism or radicalism. Eventually, however, they do mature and slough off their emotional excesses. In time their cultural and economic standards invariably improve; their numbers increase; their church property becomes aesthetic. In short, they attain a level of denominational respectability.[28]

John Mackay also describes this change when he writes, "Extravagant phenomena tend to disappear from the gathering, and the members . . . become more normal in their emotional experience."[29] In interviews with Pentecostal leaders, I sensed that this was taking place to some degree.

MAJOR THEMES OF PREACHING

A reading of the handbooks and doctrinal statements of the Pentecostals will convince one of the great emphasis placed upon redemption in the blood of Christ, the baptism and gifts of the Holy Spirit, healing, and Christ's second coming. Most of their evangelistic services combine an invitation to receive Christ as Saviour with the invitation to be healed from sickness and physical impairment.

In the questionnaire for pastors, one of the points gives a list of twelve possible themes for preaching. Each pastor was asked to check five or six of those which he chose most often for his sermons. Twenty-six pastors formed this sample, and of these, eleven were Pentecostal and fifteen were non-Pentecostal.

Table 10 is not at all inclusive, but several observations can be made from it. All eleven of the Pentecostal pastors said that the Holy Spirit was a major theme of preaching. Following this, were holiness and the second coming of Christ. Healing was mentioned by over half of the Pentecostal pastors interviewed, but was not mentioned by any of the non-Pentecostal pastors. The major themes which were chosen by the non-Pentecostal pastors were: (1) sin and repentance; (2) the consecration of the believer; (3) the mission of the church; and (4) the Holy Spirit.

From Pentecostal publications, personal observation, and the above sampling, we may conclude that the following con-

TABLE 10

MAJOR THEMES OF PREACHING CHOSEN BY A SAMPLE OF
TWENTY-SIX PASTORS

THEME	PENTECOSTAL	NON-PENTECOSTAL
Holy Spirit	11	9
Holiness	10	7
Christ's second coming	10	6
Sin and repentance	9	13
Blood of Christ	8	7
Healing	6	0
Duty of witnessing to others	6	8
Mission of the church	6	9
Consecration of the believer	2	14
Church	0	5
Creation	0	0
Tithes and offerings	0	5

stitute the major themes of Pentecostal preaching in Colombia:
(1) salvation through the blood of Christ; (2) the Holy Spirit's
work and manifestations in the believer; (3) the second coming
of Christ, with emphasis upon the contemporary fulfillment of
signs and the interpretation of events; (4) healing, which is
provided in the atonement of Christ, and which is transmitted
to the sick person through the power of the Holy Spirit. Some
Pentecostal groups, such as the Jesus Only, believe that much
sickness comes from the devil and demons, or that it is caused
by sin in the believer's life. But all may find healing—by con-
fession, if necessary—and by exercising sufficient faith in God
and His healing power.

STRICT SEPARATION FROM THE WORLD AND ITS WAYS

In their standards of dress and behavior, in their attitude to
common forms of entertainment, and in the extent to which
they generally abstain from the affairs of society and the community, Pentecostals are more separated and otherworldly
than other Protestants. For most Pentecostals in Colombia, it
it is wrong for the woman to cut her hair or use makeup. Any

music which is not strictly Christian (i.e., hymns) should not be listened to. Not only are drinking, dancing, and movies wrong, but the majority also reject entertainment in the form of drama, clubs, and sporting events such as soccer.* The United Pentecostal Church condemns television in the home, and in the matters already mentioned, is the strictest of all the Pentecostal churches.

> We disapprove completely of our people taking part in any activity which is not conducive to good Christian and godly living, namely attendance at theatres, dances, or mixed bathing; the cutting of their hair by the women or the wearing of make-up or any apparel that immodestly exposes the body; all worldly sports and entertainments; and radio and musical programs that are not wholesome. . . . We disapprove of any of our believers having television sets in their homes. We warn all of our believers to abstain from any of these practices in the interest of spiritual growth and the soon coming of the Lord for His Church.[30]

While all of the non-Pentecostal churches interviewed encourage a certain amount of involvement by believers in community, cultural, and political affairs, most of the Pentecostals —especially those of the Jesus Only churches—felt that the believer should not get "mixed up" in any of these matters.†

THE JESUS ONLY CHURCH

The United Pentecostal Church deviates from the other Pentecostal denominations that we are considering in a number of its beliefs. The first is in its doctrine that water baptism must be administered in the name of only the Lord Jesus Christ. This belief was born in a worldwide Pentecostal camp meeting held in California in 1913. At that time, a Pentecostal leader named John G. Scheppe, impressed by the miracles and heal-

---

*These convictions were brought out in the questionnaire for pastors as well as the questionnaire for members, in the sections dealing with standards. See Appendix.

†Again, this is brought out in the questionnaires for pastors and members, in the sections on standards.

ings which were taking place "in the name of Jesus," believed
he received a new revelation from God concerning "the name."

> To be sure, the "revelation" impressed many, and they has-
> tened to examine the Bible for what teaching it contained
> regarding the "name of Jesus." Their research produced a
> revolution within Pentecostalism, for they fastened upon two
> texts—Acts 2:38 and John 3:5—and asserted that *true* bap-
> tism *must* be only "in the name of Jesus" rather than "in the
> name of the Father, and of the Son, and of the Holy Ghost."
> The result? Many of the early Pentecostal leaders . . . ac-
> cepted the new "revelation" and were rebaptized. This
> created numerous divisions among Pentecostals as some sup-
> ported this view and others denounced it as rank heresy.[31]

In a booklet on doctrine published by the United Pentecostal
Church in Spanish, Oscar Vouga writes:

> The apostles, by example as well as by precept, taught us
> that we should baptize in the name of the Lord Jesus Christ
> for the remission of sins. There is no remission of sins in any
> other name than that of Christ (Acts 4:12). Therefore bap-
> tism does not mean that the believer receives remission of sins
> unless the name of the Lord is used as the baptismal formula.
> Neither can we be identified with Him in His death and resur-
> rection unless the name of Jesus is invoked upon the repentant
> one.[32]

The UPC also holds that there is only one Person in the Godhead—Jesus Christ. This was the next step in the new "revelation" in 1913 of the "name of Jesus."

> The next development in this controversy, which received
> the title "The New Issue" or the "Jesus Only" heresy, was a
> denial of the Trinity. Men like Frank Ewert and Glenn A.
> Cook, spokesman for the new teaching, denied the trinity of
> persons in the Godhead, maintaining that while God is a three-
> fold Being, Father, Son, and Holy Spirit, there is but one
> Person and that one is Jesus. . . . Its emphasis on the name of
> Jesus, the seemingly supernatural method of its being re-
> vealed, and its promise of additional power to all who ac-

cepted it, . . . accounts for the rapid spread of the theory among Pentecostals.³³

United Pentecostals emphasize texts such as Isaiah 7:14, Matthew 1:21, and John 10:30, in seeking to give a biblical foundation to their belief that there is but one divine Person— Jesus Christ—and the Father and the Holy Spirit are but manifestations of Christ Himself. On the cover of the UPC monthly publication in Colombia, "El Heraldo de la Verdad," is the theme-text: "Hear, O Israel, the LORD our God is one LORD (Deu 6:4)." Emphasis is made on John 10:30, where Christ says, "I and my Father are one." For this reason the United Pentecostals are often referred to as the Jesus Only people, or "the people of the name."

Then, there are actually three steps in salvation for the Jesus Only people: (1) repentance and faith in Christ; (2) baptism by immersion in the name of Jesus; and (3) the baptism of the Holy Spirit.

> The basic and fundamental doctrine of this organization shall be the biblical model of complete salvation, that consists of repentance, baptism in water by immersion in the name of the Lord Jesus Christ, and the baptism of the Holy Spirit with the initial sign of speaking in other tongues as the Spirit gives utterance.³⁴

According to this, all three of these experiences are necessary for complete salvation. Simply believing in Christ and repenting of one's sins is not enough: it is necessary also to be baptized "in the name," and to experience the baptism of the Holy Spirit and speaking in tongues, if one is to be completely saved. Of the Pentecostal denominations in Colombia, the United Pentecostals are the only ones that proclaim and believe in a three-phase salvation.

5

Principal Factors in the Growth of the Pentecostal Churches in Colombia

Why are the Pentecostal churches growing much faster in Colombia than the other Protestant denominations? What are the principal factors—methodological, sociological, and theological—in their superior growth? Those interested primarily in methodology may attribute Pentecostal growth to their methods only, while those interested in sociology, to sociological factors alone. Most of the Pentecostals themselves would claim that the *main* reason for their superior growth lies neither in methodological nor sociological factors, but rather in their having more of the fullness and power of the Holy Spirit in their lives, ministries, and churches. For they believe that while we preach and practice only a partial gospel, they have the "full gospel," which places special emphasis on the supernatural power and charismatic gifts of the Holy Spirit. Then on the other side of the spectrum, some evangelical leaders dismiss Pentecostal growth as a passing phenomenon due only to the emotionalism of the Latin people, and refuse to learn any lesson from this growth.

There are several main reasons why we want to find the principal factors in the growth of the Pentecostal churches in Colombia. First of all, we must explain their superior growth in the clearest way possible, since it has implications for us in other Protestant churches experiencing smaller growth. We also want to know how much of Pentecostal growth is healthy,

82

and how much of it might be less than viable. Finally, and most important, we want to put our finger on the specific factors which can help to lead the rest of us of the evangelical churches in Colombia and Latin America, to greater church growth.

ASSEMBLIES OF GOD

The Assemblies of God is the fastest-growing Protestant church in Bogota, as we noted in chapter 3. It all began with the arrival of the Harry Bartels in Bogota in 1955, and the formulation of a definite goal and strategy from the very beginning for the work in that city. The goal: to establish one hundred local churches in greater Bogota. But how could this be accomplished, and what was the basic strategy to be used?

The city of Bogota extends considerably to the north and south; so it was decided to begin the work by establishing two strong churches, one in the northern and the other in the southern part of the city. These would then become the bases from which the work could expand and other churches be planted throughout the city.

The south church—Bethel—was founded by the Bartels in 1956, through an evangelistic campaign and literature distribution and visitation. With the converts from these efforts, the church was started with a nucleus of about twenty believers. The Bethel Church grew so that by 1960 there were 70 baptized members and approximately 220 in attendance in Sunday school. In 1971 it was the largest Assemblies of God church in Bogota with 270 members and an attendance of 450. The meeting place was packed out when I attended this church in 1971.

As the south church grew and became better organized, the Bartels turned their attention to starting another church in the northern part of the city. In 1959, meetings were begun in the Bartels' home with about ten people, and later, as the congregation grew, a house was rented for the meetings. The church continued to grow, and by 1965 there were approximately 100 members and over 200 in attendance in the main services. By

1969, membership had increased to 125 and attendance to 250.

CAMPO BLANCO PLAN

But the real story in the growth of the Assemblies of God in Bogota is in the development of the *campo blanco* (whitened field) system. This is the basic strategy by which the goal of planting one hundred churches in this city is to be realized. The *campo blanco* is defined as a "place where there is a nucleus of believers and regular weekly services, with the intent that this become an organized local church."[1] Each *campo blanco* is under the direction of the organized local church which has founded it, and which oversees it until it in turn becomes an organized church.

The *campo* must have a minimum of ten baptized members to consider organizing as a local church, but there are other considerations as well, such as: how many different families are represented in the new congregation? What is the economic feasibility of the *campo* becoming an organized church? As Glen Kramer pointed out, "You can cut the umbilical cord too soon."[2] The nucleus of believers in a *campo* should also be able to show that they can financially support their pastor under terms acceptable to him, and that they can successfully maintain regular church services on their own. When a *campo* meets these basic requirements, the believers may make an official request to the General Presbitery for official approval to organize as a local church.

The basic philosophy of the *campo blanco* system is that "each local church is responsible for the territory half way to the next organized church."[3] It does not always work out exactly this way, since this is the ideal, but this does give the basic idea underlying the system. What is important for us to see here is how the *campo blanco* plan has worked out in practice in Bogota, and what it promises to accomplish in the coming years.

Since its founding in 1956, and up till 1971, the south Bethel Church had founded thirteen churches—ten of them in Bogota

—through the *campo blanco* system. The north church founded six new churches in twelve years (1959-71)—five of them in north Bogota. Yet this is but the beginning of the potential for church multiplication, for the fifteen daughter churches founded by the two central churches are now overseeing and starting other *campos blancos*.

Two churches whose pastors I interviewed that had been founded by the Bethel Church are the churches in the *barrios* Ciudad Kennedy and Bello Horizonte. Meetings were begun in Ciudad Kennedy in 1964, and the church was organized in 1965 with thirty-five members and an attendance of eighty in Sunday school. By 1969 this church had grown to almost one hundred members and an average attendance of 210. The pastor, Gustavo Quiroga, was converted in the Bethel Church, worked up as an active layman there, was named to direct the *campo blanco* work in Ciudad Kennedy, and became the pastor there when it was organized as a local church. Today the Ciudad Kennedy Church sponsors four *campos blancos,* directed by lay leaders from this church.[4]

The Bello Horizonte *campo blanco* was begun in 1966 under the leadership of Pedro Ramirez, also a convert and member of the Bethel Church. In 1967 it was organized as a church with twenty-five members and an attendance of fifty. By 1971 the membership had more than tripled, to eighty, and attendance to two hundred-fifty. Equally important, the Bello Horizonte Church had opened three *campos blancos* directed by deacons from the church.[5]

The same story might be told of the north church. One of its daughter churches is the La Paz Church. Founded as a *campo blanco* in 1967 with three members, it was organized as a church later in the year with forty-two members, and attendance of about eighty. Two years later, in 1969, the membership had doubled to eighty, and attendance to one hundred-fifty. Four *campos blancos* had been opened under the direction of lay leaders from the La Paz Church, who had been trained and delegated by the pastor at that time, Gonzalo Castano.[6] Glen Kramer explains the system further:

We put tremendous emphasis on opening *campos blancos* under the direction of organized local churches. . . . This is basic. If an organized church doesn't have *campos,* what's wrong? It's part of the reason for existence of that group. This system goes back to our experiences in Central America in El Salvador, and to the writings of Melvin Hodges. The Assemblies of God got going in Colombia later, and thus avoided a lot of paternalism, and has worked on the Hodges and El Salvador pattern.[7]

In 1971, the two mother churches and their fifteen daughter churches in Bogota had a total of some fifty-four *campos blancos.* These represent fifty-four potential churches, and if most of these become organized churches, the Assemblies of God will be well on its way to achieving the goal of having one hundred churches in the capital city!

EFFECTIVE LEADERSHIP TRAINING SYSTEM

We have stated the long-term goal of the Assemblies of God in Bogota, and their basic strategy for achieving this goal through the *campo blanco* system. But we must also mention the method of leadership that makes the *campo blanco* system workable. This method of leadership is the selection, preparation, proving, and promotion of lay leaders in each organized church, so that they may direct *campos blancos,* and lead these to growth and organization as local churches.

Ideally, each local church is not only to open *campos* in the surrounding *barrios* or neighboring towns, but is also to choose and prepare lay leaders from its ranks that can lead the *campos* to growth, and then pastor them as they become churches. Assemblies of God leader Glen Kramer emphasized:

When leaders are Spirit-led, they are led into the harvest. We need spiritual men with a vision for expansion, with the first priority of following the leading of the Holy Spirit. You can never go beyond your national leaders. . . . . As long as missionaries were leading, we had two strong churches with some outstations, but real growth came when the nationals developed as leaders for *campos blancos* and developed them into churches.[8]

How are leaders prepared for leading *campos blancos* and churches within the Assemblies of God? There are actually four steps of preparation and promotion.

Obrero local. This first step of training within the Assemblies of God is very practical and effective, and provides most of the workers and leaders for the *campos.* A believer that is faithful and active in a local church, and shows potential as a soul-winner and leader, may enroll in a series of prescribed studies given in the local church under the direction of the pastor. These include studies on: (1) the doctrines of the Assemblies of God; (2) the administration of local churches; (3) ministries in the local church, in personal evangelism and in *campos blancos;* (4) the baptism of the Holy Spirit; (5) the constitution of the Assemblies of God in Colombia; and (6) prayer in the life and ministry of the preacher and leader.

Upon successful completion of these studies, a layman becomes an *obrero local,* or "local worker," and qualifies to direct a *campo blanco.* Clearly, the requirements and course of preparation in this first step in the ministry have some very practical advantages: (1) the layman involved must first prove himself as a soul-winner and active member and leader in his own local church; (2) the training is open to potential leaders of any age or financial situation; (3) the training is local-church oriented; it is given in the local church under the direction of the local pastor, and aims at training people to begin new churches; and (4) the courses themselves emphasize Assemblies of God doctrine, church administration, and procedures, thus building geater morale, allegiance, and uniformity of goals and beliefs in its leaders.

Christian preacher. The training at this level now comes under the direction of the Bible institute in Bogota. Only those who are already local workers qualify, and most of these are directing *campos blancos* or organized churches. For those living outside of Bogota that cannot attend the Bible institute, some of the courses can be taken by correspondence. For those in Bogota who cannot attend regular classes during the day, night classes may be taken. The whole system is flexible, geared to the needs of the local churches, and to giving training to proven leaders on the job. The whole philosophy of training is expressed in these words, "We feel that a student should be called before going to the Bible institute to study, and that the local church should be his proving ground, not the Bible institute."[9]

Licensed minister. This step is for those who have proven themselves successful at leading a church to growth, and confers the authority to baptize and administer the Lord's Supper. Again, there is a prescribed series of Bible institute courses that must be taken to achieve this level in the ministry.

Ordained minister. This final step in the Assemblies of God ministerial training and promotion is for those who are proven and successful pastors of experience, maturity, and leadership, and who have finished the complete Bible institute courses. The major officials of the council of churches must be ordained (superintendent, vice-superintendent, secretary, and treasurer).[10]

No other Protestant denomination that I interviewed had such a clearly stated and outlined course of preparation and training for the ministry as the Assemblies of God, and very few have such a definite purpose and strategy in mind in training their leaders—that of multiplying local churches through the *campo blanco* system.

EXTENDED-CAMPAIGN METHOD

In 1967, the Everett Divines arrived in the city of Cali. They had already worked for a number of years with the Assemblies of God in Chile. And just as in the case of the Bartels in Bogota, they had a long-range goal in mind for the whole Valle and Caldas regions, and a strategy to carry out their goal. The goal in this case: to plant at least one Assemblies of God church in every city in the *Departamentos* of the Valle and Caldas.[11]

The strategy used to accomplish this has been the extended evangelistic campaign along with the portable tabernacle system. We have already seen how the Assemblies of God churches were planted in two of the case-study cities—Pereira and Palmira—by this method.

Generally, an outside evangelist from the Assemblies of God —national or missionary—is invited to preach during the initial campaign in a new city, and the duration of the campaign is from two to four weeks. A national, who may be a lay leader or a pastor, takes part in the initial campaign, both in the meetings and in visiting the new converts. This national will stay on after the campaign to pastor the new congregation. The meetings themselves are generally held nightly in an available vacant lot in the area where the new church is to be planted. As people make decisions, they are visited during the days of the campaign, and by the end of the campaign, are enrolled in a baptismal class to study Assemblies of God doctrines, standards, and local church policies. These new converts, when baptized, become the first members of the newly formed church.

The vacant lot used for the campaign is close to another lot which has been picked out and purchased for the building of a portable tabernacle. While the campaign is going on and people are coming to Christ, a portable tabernacle is going up nearby, and is to be ready for the new congregation to move into by the time the campaign is over. This can be illustrated in the planting of an Assemblies of God church in the city of Armenia, near Pereira.

> In Armenia, we used our basic plan. A lot was purchased before the campaign ended near the campaign site. We started building the portable tabernacle during the campaign, and it was ready for meetings a week after the campaign ended.[12]

The portable tabernacles are made out of inexpensive, prefabricated sections that can be put up very quickly, and can be dismantled when the church is ready to build a larger and more permanent structure.

This method of planting churches is working. The first Assemblies of God church founded by this method in this region was in a *barrio* of Cali, in 1967. By 1971—four years later—seven new churches had been planted in this way in six towns and cities of the Valle and Caldas regions. All of these churches have national pastors and are self-supporting. The only resident Assemblies of God missionaries in this region of Colombia have been the Divines. In an interview with Everett Divine, he gave me what he considers the main ingredients for this church-planting strategy: (1) definite reliance on the Holy Spirit; (2) working with a national from the very start of the campaign, who will take over the direction of the new church; (3) the extended evangelistic campaign itself along with the follow-up of new converts; and (4) the portable tabernacle system. About this last point Divine says, "I've played with renting rooms for meetings, but it doesn't work. The best way is to buy a property and get a roof over their heads for their meetings."[13]

So the Assemblies of God in Colombia have an effective way of planting new churches through the extended-campaign method, and of multiplying existing churches through the *campo blanco* system. And they have a practical and effective way to prepare local church lay leaders to pastor the new churches through the *obrero local* system of training. In an interview with Ed Murphy, past director of Overseas Crusades in Colombia, he summed up the success of the Assemblies of God in this country in this way:

1. The churches are organized for church planting in the *barrios*. I was in the Bethel Church in Bogota for a series of conferences especially for lay leaders and "Christian preachers." The pastor, Octavio Moreno, required that these leaders attend the conferences. Roll was taken, and the leaders were given an exam. The place was jammed with two hundred-fifty to three hundred leaders, and the emphasis was on training leaders for opening and directing *campos blancos*.

2. They have the implicit belief that the church is a mission agency and the Christian a witness. I was in an Assemblies of God church in Bogota in *barrio* Kennedy. The place was filled, and there was standing room only. A lot of members brought new people. When some made decisions, the mem-

bers of the church were ready to deal with them; these members are mobilized.

3. They have a pastoral training program which is immensely practical. To me, their program of training leaders for the churches is the closest to the New Testament ideal that I've seen in our day.[14]

PANAMERICAN MISSION

We have already seen that the Panamerican church is one of the youngest and fastest growing in Colombia. In the city of Pereira, it is second in its rate of growth among the denominations there; and in Bogota, it very likely would be as large as the Assemblies of God today if it had not been for the church split which took place there in the late sixties.

Some evangelical leaders feel that the Panamerican church has the best possibilities for growth in the coming years, of any of the Trinitarian Pentecostal denominations. Ruperto Velez is a Colombian leader with Overseas Crusades, and has visited and observed all the major Trinitarian Pentecostal churches in Colombia. When I asked him which of these, in his opinion, has most life, most momentum, and the best prospects for growth in the future, he replied, "The Panamerican Mission." He then added:

> It seems to me that Ignacio Guevara is seeking to throw off the traditions of other denominations, but at the same time is seeking to put Bible teachings into practice in the church. They are using their leaders where they have gifts and can best serve. They are placing the members of the body where they can function the best.[15]

I sensed this myself as I had interviews with some of the Panamerican leaders and pastors. If the Panamerican Mission can avoid excesses in the charismatic manifestations, the wrong kind of men at the top, and the kind of split that hurt them so badly in Bogota, they have some advantages and ways of working that could give them very strong growth in the coming years. Some of the advantages and factors in growth of the Panamerican Mission are these: (1) it is a very new movement and not tied to denominational traditions; (2) it is a completely national and indigenous church; (3) it has strong leadership; (4) it is using effective methods of evangelism and church planting.

The fact that the Panamerican Mission is new and not tied to denominational traditions also includes the dangers of instability and inexperience. But its newness does give the Panamerican Mission the opportunity to set up its organizational structure, its strategy, and its way of working, in a way which seems best in the Colombian situation. This young indigenous church is free to innovate and try new things more easily than the denominations tied to years of tradition and fixed ways of doing things.

> Organizationally, the Panamerican church has a very New Testament structure. Guevara acts as an apostle, and he has several men that act in the same capacity. Others serve as pastors-teachers, prophets, etc. When Guevara and the other leaders see something as biblical, they do it. The structure is loose enough so that they can change when they need to; it is a very flexible structure.[16]

And the Panamerican Mission is innovating. One example of this is an interesting plan or experiment that has been initiated in Bogota, and which is a model for the whole country. There are six Panamerican churches in the capital, with five pastors and one young man that serve full-time in these churches. Hector Machuca, the pastor of the central church, oversees all six pastors and churches, and visits them regularly. When I asked Machuca how he works with the other pastors and how the churches in Bogota are governed, he replied,

> The pastors and leaders of the six churches meet with me each Wednesday morning. We pray, have a Bible study, discuss pending matters, and divide the work to be done in the churches. We don't want any pastor to get so stuck in one church, or the churches to get so attached to one pastor that he can't move, so we rotate continually.
>
> Business sessions in our churches used to be times of discouragement, differences, and divisions. Now, instead of an

official board in the churches, we have the ministerial board made up of the pastors and leaders of the six churches. This board takes care of serious matters in the churches and work; minor matters are taken care of by the pastors and their local church deacons.[17]

In the Panamerican churches in Bogota, the tithes and offerings go to the Bogota general fund. All *tithes* are for the support of pastors and ministers, since the Panamerican leaders are convinced that 100 percent of tithes should go for ministries, whether in a local church, new work, or to the churches in Colombia in general. "We believe in dedicating church tithes to the support of the pastor and ministries, not buildings, because the pastor is more important than a building. A church can be in a home."[18] The offerings that come in over and above the tithes are used to pay for utilities, literature, and evangelistic efforts in the churches. Funds for church buildings are raised with special offerings taken up in all the churches, until the amount needed is raised. The *tithe* of offerings (not tithes) goes to a rotating fund especially for establishing new works.

Not all of the tithes from the Bogota churches go for the support of the local pastors, as Hector Machuca explains:

> We help one brother in Medellin who has the gift of prophecy in the churches, a pastor in a new work in Ibague, and two evangelists that live in Bogota, but serve in all the churches. In all we help to support sixteen ministers, including the six pastors here. For me, the system we have adopted for leadership and support, is the best that we could have.[19]

Ignacio Guevara, founder and "apostle" of the Panamerican church, explained what they consider to be the biblical ministerial system: "We place emphasis on the five ministerial gifts of Ephesians 4:11-12: apostolic, prophetic, evangelistic, pastoral, and of teaching. This we call the 'hand of Christ.' "[20] The Panamerican leaders feel that each pastor or leader has one of these gifts and has proven it, and that those having a ministry to the whole church in Colombia should be adequately supported and freed to carry out this ministry. Some of these serve as apostles, opening new churches, some as evangelists, and others as prophets and teachers. This system has produced a high morale in the Panamerican pastors and leaders and a more complete ministry to the churches.

The Panamerican Mission is not tied to any foreign mission or denomination. Guevara, the leaders, and all the pastors are Colombians. This church is the closest of any of the Trinitarian Protestant denominations in Colombia to being a self-supporting, self-governing, and self-propagating national church.

This has some advantages. For one thing, when there are problems, the Colombian leaders must face them squarely themselves, and not look to a foreign mission for the solution. The pastors may not have very high salaries, but the Panamerican leaders have tried to find a solution to this problem in the way which seems best to them. And as we have seen, this is exactly what they have done with a fair amount of success.

> It is a church that is in the hands of the nationals from the top down. The church as a whole receives very little help from the outside, and all the local churches are self-supporting. Because it is a national church, there are less bad feelings over finances.[21]

And of course, because it is a national church, the leaders can make it as Colombian as they want to; there are no outsiders to impose their ideas as to how things ought to be done.

Another plus factor for the Panamerican mission is its strong leadership. Guevara has been a strong but good leader. He enjoys far more authority as the founder and director of the Panamerican Mission, than do the leaders of other denominations. He is really the final leader with the final say. Fortunately, Guevara has proven to be a spiritual, capable, and sensible leader, ready to make changes in the mission and its policies if it seems necessary, or if he feels that there has been a mistaken emphasis in the churches.

Though Guevara is a strong leader, he does not stifle the development of other leaders. "Guevara is a *caudillo,* a figurehead, and a strong, sensible leader. But he is not a dictator. He recognizes and encourages gifts and leadership in others."[22] He is also known as a man of vision, prayer, and unceasing activity in the work of Christ. These same qualities he wants to instill in other Panamerican pastors and leaders, and continually warns against any spirit of professionalism in the ministry.

> There is a certain pastoral professionalism where men seek to live off the ministry without a passion for souls. . . . We need a spiritual renewal in the Christian ministry to a life of true consecration, of sacrifice, of prayer, of passion for souls. There is a lack of vision in too many ministers.[23]

So Guevara's leadership and vision have been a major factor in the growth and development of the Panamerican Mission.

In the Panamerican churches, the pastor also has more authority than his counterparts in the non-Pentecostal churches, or even in the Assemblies of God churches. He is the final leader and has the final say as to the naming of deacons, how the church's money is to be spent, the activities of the church, and so on. Guevara gave this concept of the pastor and his authority:

> The pastor is a leader placed in the ministry by God. He should take the direction of the church 100 percent. The church should not run the pastor. The Lord gave gifts to the pastor, and when the church runs him, it is like a car steering the driver. The pastor, not a board of officials, should take the direction of the church.[24]

Guevara considers this system of pastoral authority to be one of the factors in their growth. Hector Machuca, the overseer in Bogota, agrees, and says that there were problems, and dissensions in the churches of Bogota until the pastors' role was changed, giving them the authority to make decisions on all important church matters. But this, of course, also has its pros and cons, according to Ed Murphy:

> The whole concept of the pastor is in many respects the *caudillo* concept. But these *caudillo* pastors are really natural

and gifted leaders because of the apprenticeship system of
developing leaders. The danger is that some men may rise
up in a church where the pastor doesn't allow their development.[25]

Since the pastors are almost always the accepted and chosen
leaders of the believers themselves, and have proven themselves in their ministries and churches, they have in one sense
earned authority for themselves. And as long as they are good
and spiritual leaders, the *caudillo* system can work, since the
people are accustomed to this leadership pattern.

> The growing Pentecostals are intensely indigenous. . . .
> They freely adopt and adapt practices and procedures in
> church life which reflect their cultural background and heri-
> tage. Ecclesiastical structures are modified to suit Latin
> American patterns. Whether polity is officially congregational,
> presbyterian, or episcopal (and all three types are present),
> the structure always seems to evolve to a pattern of strong
> personal leadership, which is the pattern most understand-
> able to Latin Americans.[26]

METHODS

Home Bible-study groups, directed by laymen. One of the
newer and more effective means of outreach of the Panamerican Mission is through Bible studies in homes. In Bogota,
besides having seven branch preaching points with regular
services, the churches are conducting numerous Bible studies
in homes through the members. These become soul-winning
centers that feed new believers to the churches.

In Medellin, Ignacio Guevara is very excited about what is
happening through this method of outreach:

> We are tired of trying to bring people to the church. So
> we are going to their homes, almost in the fashion of the
> Jehovah's Witnesses. Every week we meet in different homes.
> We don't sing any hymns, because the new people are not
> accustomed to hymns and would get frightened off. So we
> just open the meeting to the study of the Bible. . . . We began
> a year and a half ago, and now we meet in eleven homes

weekly. Many neighbors are attending these Bible studies, and entire families are being converted to Christ.[27]

The whole idea of this method is to multiply the outreach of the churches in the cities by mobilizing and using as many members as possible to foment and direct these Bible studies.

> Their whole concept of the church's ministry is that of Ephesians 4:11-12: training the saints to evangelize and do the work of the ministry. I was in a small Panamerican church in Medellin. The pastor said, "We're in a probing ministry to find out where there are interested people. Who will offer their homes for services?" Four men offered to do so, and were named to direct the meetings in their homes. Neighbors would be invited in. The whole thing was flexibly structured, and the members realized that *they,* not the pastor, were the ones who would direct these efforts in the different points.[28]

Branch outstations directed by lay leaders. This is well illustrated in the case of the founding, development, and outreach of the Panamerican church in Pereira.

Segundo Tellez, who had been a traffic policeman, was converted in Bogota under the ministry of Ignacio Guevara, and received training under him as a lay leader in the central church there. In 1960 Segundo was sent by Ignacio to begin a new church from scratch in Pereira. As the church in Pereira grew, Segundo in turn taught and prepared lay leaders who could direct new outreach efforts. When the Pereira church opened a new work in the town of Pueblo Rico, Eleazar Londono was sent to direct this work. Now Eleazar has twenty-five preaching points in homes and settlements in the region around Pueblo Rico. So four steps of outreach are represented in this chain of church-planting: Bogota—Pereira—Pueblo Rico—twenty-five preaching points in the Pueblo Rico region.

The Pereira church has also started new churches in the towns of Salamina and Cairo, in the same region. Both of these churches have been built up and directed by lay leaders from the Pereira church.

Actually the Pereira church is even responsible for planting

a new church far off in the eastern Amazon jungles in the out-
post town of Leticia. A leading believer of the Pereira church,
named Benhur, moved to Leticia, opened a small store there,
and began meetings in his home. After he had won several
people to Christ, some of these also began to win others in the
area. Ignacio Guevara describes the process:

> We had a meeting recently in Leticia to baptize eight con-
> verts of Benhur. Segundo Tellez went in with me. We found
> that one of Benhur's converts is now evangelizing the Indians
> along the rivers, and ten of the converts have been baptized.
> So five spiritual generations were represented there: myself,
> Segundo, Benhur, the eight won to Christ by Benhur, and
> the ten Indians won to Christ by one of Benhur's converts.[29]

Whenever this kind of process is taking place, churches are
bound to reproduce and grow, and it is just this process that
accounts for much of the growth of the Panamerican church.
Lay leaders are trained, open new works, become pastors, and
begin to train their own lay leaders for further new outreach
efforts. This is the process of reproduction and multiplication!

The Panamerican Mission has no formal Bible institute
of its own, and few of its pastors have had any formal theological training. In this respect, the Assemblies of God has a
much more thorough and defined system of preparation for its
pastors and leaders. But the Panamerican pastors and leaders
do meet periodically for fellowship, planning, and Bible study,
usually in Medellin or Bogota. And now a beginning has also
been made in giving more definite preparation to leaders that
are coming up, because, as Guevara says, "We saw that there
was a lack of teaching the Word to our workers. Consequently,
we have begun studies in Medellin for prospective pastors and
leaders."[30]

The students accepted for study in Medellin are lay leaders
who are already serving and preaching in their own local
churches and outstations, and who have been approved as
prospective pastors and workers. The courses are very informal,

with the predominant emphasis on the study of the Bible itself. The course lasts for four months, in two divided periods of two months each. But it is not a formal, organized Bible institute by any means, and graduation to the ministry is still on the basis of the apprenticeship system. "Graduation with us is different. We see the work that a Christian leader does, and with time, experience, and fruit, the laying on of hands may come."[31]

There are three defined steps of promotion for a worker in the Panamerican Mission: (1) a lay preacher in a local church or outstation; (2) a licensed preacher, who is one that has proven himself as a lay leader and is in charge of a church. If a licensed preacher is not very active and does not see growth in his church, he will remain at this level in the ministry; (3) ordained preacher. When a licensed preacher is a good leader, faithful, and successful in leading a congregation to growth, his case is taken before the leaders of the Panamerican Mission, who decide after prayer and consideration whether the man in question is worthy of ordination.

> The essential emphasis in the training of leaders is practical experience, instead of purely academic preparation. Yet some of their men are sharp. . . . The emphasis is on-the-job training, and Ignacio Guevara, the founder, has himself given the example in this. Some of the present pastors and leaders were converts of Ignacio and he trained them and gave them a vision for the work. These have gone on to found new churches.[32]

Guevara sums up his strategy for church growth in this way: "Every believer ought to win others; every pastor ought to train others; and every church ought to plant other churches."[33]

INTERNATIONAL CHURCH OF THE FOURSQUARE GOSPEL

The Foursquare church is so named because of the four points which they emphasize in their preaching: salvation, baptism in the Holy Spirit, healing, and the second coming of Christ. This "perfect" (foursquare) gospel is for them the only answer to man's every need, "complete for body, soul, spirit, and for eternity."[34]

The Foursquare church is the largest of the Trinitarian Pentecostal denominations in Colombia, though its rate of growth is not as high as that of the Assemblies of God or the Panamerican Mission. At the time this study was being done, there was no Foursquare church in any of the three case-study cities, but from interviews with a number of leaders who have observed the Foursquare churches firsthand, these factors emerge as primary in their growth.

BRANCH SUNDAY SCHOOLS

While the Assemblies of God have multiplied churches through the *campo blanco* system, many of the Foursquare churches have emphasized branch Sunday schools. Murphy reports, "There are *anexos* all over the place, and on Sunday morning these branch Sunday schools are taken over by laymen."[35] Ruperto Velez describes a service he attended and the activity he witnessed in this church:

> In 1968 I was in the largest church in Barranquilla. There were between nine hundred and one thousand people in the Sunday school. When the morning service was over, the church register showed more than two thousand in attendance, because they had brought the attendance data from all the branch Sunday schools that the church oversees in the *barrios* of the city. These Sunday schools are under the central church, and are directed by members of the central church.[36]

EVANGELISTIC OUTREACH THROUGH THE MEMBERS

Speaking again of the largest Foursquare church in the city of Barranquilla, Ed Murphy says,

> There is tremendous evangelistic outreach in visitation and open-air preaching. There are some four hundred believers that come out every Saturday afternoon for evangelistic visitation. No one can sing in the choir unless he first participates in this activity.[37]

5 1 6 3 4.

Humberto Blandon, a representative with the Bible societies in Colombia, considers the Foursquare church in the city of Cucuta, on the Venezuelan border, as one of the most exceptional in growth in Colombia. In 1964 there were just a few believers in this church in its beginnings: by 1970 there were over eight hundred. One of the reasons Blandon gives for this growth is "the use of laymen in preaching and directing in the main temple itself, in preaching points, and in visitation evangelism." He then adds:

> This church has founded six congregations in the city and others in the surrounding areas. The church sends lay preachers and pastors to other points outside the city to begin new churches, and these are supported by the main church itself.[38]

The Foursquare church in the city of Barrancabermeja is one of their oldest and largest churches in Colombia. When I interviewed a leader from this church in 1970, he gave the attendance as being over 1,000 in the main service. Some of the evangelistic activities of the church that he mentioned were regular weekly jail visitation, preaching services every week in six different *barrios* of the city, and a church outreach which extends to a number of neighboring villages and towns, where services are held weekly as well. His own attitude, typical of so many Pentecostals, is of willingness and desire to witness and evangelize:

> We have a wrought-iron furniture business. I can do much of my work in half a day, and this leaves me time for the work of the Lord. . . . I like to encourage and build up the congregations outside of the city that need help. . . . Sometimes the pastor calls me and says, "Why don't you take a few brethren and visit this town and have a service there." . . . Many of the brethren of the church serve and evangelize with wilingness and enthusiasm. Every believer ought to feel this desire; it is normal.[39]

But the most interesting part of my interview with Uriel Trejos, was hearing of the plan his church has to mobilize *every* believer through evangelistic teams. Each team is to have a different type of ministry and outreach, and each believer is to be placed on the team where it is felt that he can do the best job. Each team would be responsible for one of these ministries: door-to-door evangelism; open-air meetings in parks and congested points in the city; cottage meetings held in the homes of members in different *barrios* of the city; visitation and prayer for the sick.

LAY-TRAINING INSTITUTES

These institutes are primarily for preparing believers to evangelize and direct branch Sunday schools and outreach efforts. "They have a very great interest in preparing and motivating every believer to develop his gifts, witness, and serve in the work."[40]

The Foursquare church in Barrancabermeja has what is termed a "Bible institute" for the preparation of church members in the work. Uriel Trejos has taken two courses—one by correspondence—and plans to take more; he says:

> I have not thought of being a pastor. I prepare myself in order to understand the Word, to preach, and to serve in the work. . . . I feel that my ministry is to go outside the city and preach to small churches. I do it on my own because I like to go to these churches where there aren't so many talents, and help out.[41]

Speaking about the Foursquare church in Cucuta, Humberto Blandon stressed that "they dedicate a lot of time to institutes for believers in general. The main purpose of these is to prepare them for personal evangelism and evangelism in outstations and preaching points."[42]

UNITED PENTECOSTAL CHURCH

The United Pentecostal Church is the largest and fastest-growing Protestant denomination in Colombia today. It is also the largest and fastest-growing Protestant church in two of the case-study cities, Pereira and Palmira. In Bogota, the other case-study city, it is second to the Assemblies of God. Because of its success, the factors in the growth of the United Pentecostal Church are especially important to us in this study.

In chapter 3, I mentioned that this is now a completely national and autonomous church. At the annual convention of the United Pentecostal Church in 1967, the Colombian leaders voted to go this way. Before this, missionaries had been in charge in many ways; but after becoming autonomous, Colombians took over all the official and administrative positions in the church. Domingo Zuniga was elected president and took on the oversight of the churches as a full-time job. The only authority of the missionaries was to give counsel when it was requested by the Colombian church. As far as the mission board in the United States is concerned, the only link was to be that of fellowship, not administration nor direction.[43] Officials of the United Pentecostal Church came from the United States and turned over church properties and funds to the official Colombian board, in the name of the church in Colombia. As for how all this changeover went, Sally Morley says, "All went smoothly, but there had been the human element as well, of ambitions and hard feelings."[44]

Later, however, the missionary reaction to all this was more pronounced. The missionaries associated with the mission board in the United States decided to break away from the Colombian church and to begin new churches on their own. These churches also carried the name "United Pentecostal Church, " but were associated with the foreign mission board. This reaction on the part of the missionaries to the complete nationalization of the church in Colombia is described by Cornelia Flora:

> The missionaries did not accept this, and their resignation was accepted. The places most affected by the split were Bogota and Meta, where the national leadership was not as strong as in other parts of Colombia, and where the Thompsons, who are particularly charismatic leaders, were located. Much bitterness surfaced at that time, and the various churches in the area were split in two, with many Colombians torn between loyalties. At the youth convention in Bogota in

August of 1969, many pastors and workers who had gone with the missionaries publicly repented and reentered the Colombian group.[45]

Because the United Pentecostal Church of Colombia is now autonomous, it has some of the advantages mentioned for the Panamerican Mission. The leaders are more free to "Colombianize," to innovate, and to utilize what they consider the best financial plan for their pastors and churches. But it has also opened the door to certain dangers, which we will mention in the next chapter.

It is interesting to note that in Latin America, it is only in Colombia that the United Pentecostal Church has had such exceptional growth compared with the other denominations. In many countries of Latin America, the largest and fastest-growing churches are Pentecostal, but they are trinitarian. Yet in Colombia, it is the Jesus Only church that has broken away from the rest of the Protestant churches, even the Pentecostal churches, in its growth. How have they achieved this? What are some of the principal factors that acount for their growth?

THE "DROST" METHOD OR PHILOSOPHY

We have already referred to the William Drosts in chapter 3, and to the growth and expansion that the Pentecostal church experienced under their ministry in the southwestern region of Colombia. The Drosts moved to Cali in 1949, and made this city the center of their efforts. Within one year, several churches had been founded, and five hundred converts baptized in Cali and in the surrounding area. After ten years, there were over twenty churches and preaching points throughout the Valle and Caldas regions as a result of the Drosts' ministry and the "method" which they introduced. The growth of the United Pentecostal Church was so rapid in this part of Colombia, that William Drost's method came to be adopted in other parts of Colombia, and became the pattern for their work in the whole country.[46]

Actually, the Drost "strategy" for the expansion of the work was largely an unplanned and spontaneous thing. Drost himself had received no formal theological training, and no special preparation in missionary procedures or strategies. He was a layman, and his main qualifications were a burden for winning souls and a very strong belief in the basic tenets of the United Pentecostal Church. As Drost won new converts to the Pentecostal faith, they were baptized "in the name," led into the experience of Holy Spirit baptism and speaking in tongues, and immediately encouraged to go and win others to the faith, with the promise that the Holy Spirit would give them supernatural power for living and witnessing victoriously.

> Refugees from the mountains came to the Pentecostal services. . . . They couldn't understand the preaching because Drost's Spanish was so bad, but he was able to play his accordion, to sing, and to show them where to read in the Bible, especially the book of Acts, which describes the first Pentecostal experience. And he was able to lead them in prayer so they received the baptism of the Holy Spirit and spoke in tongues. . . . The new believers, filled with the joy of what they had received, went back to the mountains to tell their friends and relatives what had occurred.[47]

We might call Drost's "method" that of immediate, spontaneous evangelization by new believers, and of voluntary and natural leadership. Converts with their new beliefs and experiences witnessed everywhere they went, and those who wanted to preach and teach were allowed to do so. Some of the missionaries felt it was unwise to let men preach that had received no special training for the ministry. But not Drost; after all, he was just a layman with no formal theological training, and God was using him. Why could He not do the same with the Colombian converts? And since the emphasis in the United Pentecostal Church is on a few major beliefs, and on personal and charismatic experiences, there was little need for deep or thorough theological study before beginning to preach. Besides, the people they were seeking to reach were simple people of the popular classes, who would appreciate a simple but dynamic message. Lay leaders simply preached what they had believed and experienced, and invited others to do the same.

Some of these lay preachers who showed natural leadership, and who experienced success in their ministries, became pastors of churches. The preparation of pastors came to be completely through the apprenticeship system.

> William Drost had an ideology of missionary work that differed from the classical colonial model. . . . He felt he should treat the Colombians as brethren in administrative as well as spiritual matters. He immediately designated as pastors nationals he felt were ready, although others connected with the mission doubted the wisdom of such a move. . . . Short of money, he was not notable to support a large paid staff of pastors. Evangelization occurred when people were inspired to do it for the Lord, unpaid by the missionaries. They did not become hirelings or dependent on foreign sources for funds or leadership. . . . People on fire for the Lord were used immediately, rather than stuck in an institute for four years with the possibility of emerging quite learned but spiritually dead as doorknobs. Those who wanted to preach were allowed to preach.[48]

While Drost initiated this "method" of missionary work, other United Pentecostal missionaries adopted and continued this method as they saw how successful it was in producing church growth. Sally Morley related how she and her husband felt when they first arrived in the Valle to work, and saw what was happening:

> When we came (my husband was from England and was the "old school" type), we looked around and decided that what was started was in the right direction. We decided to continue to let laymen go all over to preach, plant churches, and become pastors.[49]

Lewis Morley added that "if we have done anything, it is that we had the sense not to come in and try to dominate the movement or the churches."[50] Other Pentecostal missionaries took the same attitude and approach to the work.

> Most of our concentration was now in the Valle, but as the revival and work were going so well in the Valle, the mis-

sionaries of the "old school" in Barranquilla and other places decided to follow the same method.[51]

To this day, the United Pentecostal Church has no Bible institute or formal theological training for its pastors or leaders. There are three levels of ministry in their apprenticeship system: (1) local worker, an active lay leader that preaches under the guidance and direction of a local church and its pastor, but is not allowed to administer baptism or the Lord's Supper; (2) licensed pastor with national credentials, meaning that he can preach or pastor a church anywhere in Colombia, as well as administer the sacraments; and (3) ordained pastor. Ordination may be requested after three years as a licensed pastor. As an ordained minister, a man may now be called upon to supervise a zone and its churches and ministries. Only ordained pastors are possible candidates for serving as presbyters over the entire Colombian church.[52]

AGGRESSIVE MISSIONARY OUTREACH

Another positive aspect of the Pentecostal church's success is that it is missionary-minded. There is a continual emphasis in the local churches, and on the part of the leaders of the denomination, on establishing new churches everywhere in Colombia, and even in other countries. Because of this emphasis, the United Pentecostal Church today has churches in more *Departamentos* and points in Colombia than any other Protestant church, even in isolated regions such as the Guajira, Caqueta, Putumayo, and the Choco. It is also the only Protestant church that I know of in Colombia that has sent and supports Colombian missionaries to other countries. In 1970, this church had sent and was completely supporting nine Colombian missionaries in three other countries—Ecuador, Bolivia, and Spain. Each couple receives the equivalent of about two hundred dollars a month support, which is very good by Colombian standards.[53]

To accomplish the sending of Colombian workers and missionaries to new points within Colombia and to other countries, the United Pentecostal Church has established what is known as the *Fondo Nacional* (national fund). This fund is made up of the tithes of all the pastors and workers, the tithes of all the offerings that come in to the churches, and a monthly missionary offering which is taken up in every church.

Besides the substantial missionary giving, there is a continual missionary emphasis. Each month there is a special missionary service in every church, and this is when the monthly missionary offering is taken. Then, in the big annual convention held in one of the larger cities each year, with thousands of Jesus Only believers present, "The last day of the convention is dedicated to missions. There is a missionary message and the challenge is given to send and support Colombian missionaries in new areas of Colombia and in other countries."[54] Missions is also presented continually in their publications, especially in the monthly magazine, "El Heraldo de la Verdad" (herald of truth). Often a missionary family is featured, a letter from a missionary published, or a report given on the work in one of the new areas or foreign countries where missionaries are serving.

This whole missionary emphasis gives the idea of a dynamic church on the move, and this in itself attracts new people to the movement, and helps to create a high morale in those who are already members. Everyone likes to belong to something that is moving ahead and expanding, and this seems to be especially true in Colombia. People are drawn to the Jesus Only church because they see so much happening there, and so much growth. It is an attitude of, "God must be with them in a special way. Look at how they are going ahead." To use a cliché, "Nothing succeeds like success."

LIBERALITY IN GIVING

The United Pentecostal Church is known for the generosity of its members. In the questionnaire for members, twenty-two of the twenty-three Jesus Only members interviewed said that they tithed faithfully, "because this is the command of God." In the United Pentecostal Church, tithing is taught as a biblical command to every believer, and generous offerings are encouraged as an expression of consecration to the Lord and love for His work. As a result, the giving in this denomination is really quite exceptional, if compared to that of other churches.

In 1967, when the United Pentecostal Church had approximately 20,000 members, over 200 churches were making regular contributions to the national organization. These contributions, which were the tithes of the total offerings to these churches, totaled $383,727.68, in Colombian pesos.[55] This meant that Colombian Pentecostals in this church contributed almost four million pesos in that year—about $270,000 in American money! Now that the church has approximately 10,000 more members, and twice as many churches, this amount has likely increased considerably.

Because these Pentecostals give so liberally, there are funds available for the missionary outreach that we have just mentioned, for extending building loans to churches, for radio and literature, and for many other evangelistic efforts that other denominations in Colombia cannot afford.

The United Pentecostal churches are also quite liberal with their pastors, at least if they are large enough so they can be. Several of the Pentecostal pastors that I interviewed were receiving salaries of the equivalent of two hundred dollars per month, besides the provision of a parsonage and sometimes a vehicle. This is certainly exceptional in Colombia. Because of its large membership, and the generous giving of its people, this is a church that has money to work with.

EVERY-MEMBER EVANGELISM

Another contribution to their success is that every member is expected to be an aggressive evangelist. More than any other Protestant church that I studied, the United Pentecostal Church is known, by friends and enemies alike, for the zealous and untiring witness and evangelistic activities of its members. Gabriel Velez, a Presbyterian pastor, expressed the sentiment of many regarding the Jesus Only people:

They are all evangelists, and they have works everywhere. There are groups that hold meetings all around the city in *barrios* and in surrounding *veredas*. Often when I am returning from a service in an outlying area, I come across a group of Pentecostals either going or coming from a meeting somewhere.[56]

Domingo Zuniga, himself a leader in the United Pentecostal Church, makes the claim that "every believer you see in our churches is ready to take the gospel to anyone."[57]

A good example of this is their second church in Pereira— the Cuba Church. These are some of the activities of this one church.

Visitation teams. This church of 310 members has three teams that are organized for visitation evangelism in the *barrio* itself. Each team has about fifteen members. Two of these teams are made up of men who go on door-to-door visitation on weekends; the other team is made up of women who go out on weekdays. Their ministry is to explain the Pentecostal message, invite the people to attend the church services, and distribute New Testaments and gospel portions along with their own special tracts.

Then on Sunday afternoons, almost the whole church membership goes out on visitation to invite and bring new people to the evangelistic services in the evenings. No part of the membership is excluded from this all important activity of the church.[58]

Network of preaching points. At the time of the interview with the pastor in 1969, this church had twenty-one preaching points with a total attendance of more than 350, and this church was then only two years old!

To get a new point started, a group of members will often make an "invasion" of the town or settlement. Several taxis may be contracted to take them to the designated town in the morning. The whole day is then spent visiting and evangelizing from door to door. Often there will be an evangelistic service that evening to which all are invited. After the evangelistic ac-

tivities of the day, the taxis return to take the visiting team back
to Pereira.

Once a preaching point has been established it is assigned to
one of three evangelism teams, one made up of men, another
of women, and the third of young people. These teams are
responsible for visiting certain preaching points on a periodic
basis, and especially the people who have shown interest in the
Pentecostal faith.

Some of the preaching points have at least a weekly meeting,
and others every two weeks, depending on their size and distance from the Cuba Church. Laymen from the Cuba Church
direct most of these missions.[59]

Open-air evangelism. Frequently a large group of members
under the direction of leading laymen or the young people's
society, hold open-air meetings either at congested points in the
barrio itself, or in the nearby Matecana Park. On Sundays, this
park is often frequented by over a thousand people, as families
go to spend the day there. Then the Jesus Only people arrive
with their guitars and perhaps a loud-speaking system. Some
will sing, others give testimony, and a more capable speaker
will give the message. Then tracts and gospels are distributed
to the listeners.

The above are all organized activities of one Pentecostal
church of average size. But as important as these organized
efforts is the spontaneous personal evangelism which is continually encouraged of the members. How is this achieved?
"As pastors, we always teach and encourage the believer to
evangelize. We continually emphasize that every member—
with the power of the Holy Spirit—must witness."[60] Another
leading pastor, who is now head of the largest United Pentecostal church in Cali, said,

> The best method of winning new people has been the per-
> sonal evangelism of the believers. Some of the members of
> the church make a vow to God that they are going to bring a
> certain number of new people to the church within a certain
> period of time. Then there are others that don't bring so

many to the church meetings themselves, but do a lot of personal evangelism wherever they are.[61]

In the questionnaire for church members, fifteen out of twenty-three Jesus Only people interviewed said that they had been won to Christ primarily through the witness of other Pentecostal believers. The same members were also asked what they felt was the best and most effective way to win new people to Christ: through evangelistic campaigns, cottage meetings, visitation, or spontaneous personal evangelism by the members? Seventeen out of twenty-three answered "spontaneous personal evangelism." To the question, How often do you witness? sixteen said "constantly," five "someimes," and only two, "very seldom." The emphasis on personal evangelism by every member was stronger in the case of the United Pentecostal people interviewed, than with those of any other church.

In the United Pentecostal Church, the real "hero" is the soul winner. The believer has this goal set before him at all times, and receives the recognition of the church and its leaders when he is successful in winning new people to his faith. In a service I attended in the first Pentecostal church of Palmira, I witnessed this. The secretary of the Sunday school was invited to come up on the platform. The secretary then read the names of the believers who had brought the most new people during the past quarter, and these believers were then invited to come up on the platform. At least seven or eight of them were asked to give testimony while the rest of the congregation looked on in admiration. One teacher who was lame pointed to a pupil and said, "This girl brought eleven new ones. How many say, 'Glory to God!' " Another teacher shouted with enthusiasm, "He that wins souls is wise!" And the congregation responded with amens, for these were the heroes, worthy of praise and recognition, because they had won the most new people. This kind of service not only encouraged the ones being rewarded with the recognition of their peers, but also spurred the other members on to achieve the same thing. The pastor of this church, Jesus Cardozo, says,

Each member works in some way. But since there is a tendency for enthusiasm to wane with the passing of time, we have special Sunday school campaigns each year. During these campaigns, which last three months, the church is especially active in personal evangelism as each member determines to bring a certain number of new people to the church during the campaign. Others go from house to house throughout the area.[62]

CULTURAL APPEAL

In Colombian terminology, we would say that this church is *criolla,* meaning, of the land and of the people. This also goes back in large part to Drost, who simply let the new believers and national leaders do things in their own way as they thought best. The natural result of this was church services and ways of expressing their faith that were very Colombian. "Drost gave the people freedom to work and evangelize, not imposing rules or methods, allowing them to innovate to fit Colombian cultural needs."[63] One of the reasons that Sally Morley gives for the growth of the United Pentecostal Church is this:

The church that developed has been very indigenous and Colombian from the beginning, at least in the Valle. The Colombian believers were allowed to do things in their own way. If they wanted to paint a church red and pink—fine.[64]

When I asked the Morleys why they thought some of the other churches grew so slowly, they answered, "Their services do not appeal as much to the Colombians. They are too North American."[65]

One of the major expressions of any culture is its music, and the Pentecostals make full use of Colombian rhythms and beats. The *pasillo,* the *danza,* and the *bolero* are popular rhythms in Colombia, and they are heard frequently in the Jesus Only churches. In their meetings, one will also hear, not only pianos, guitars, and accordions, but also maracas and tambourines. In fact, Sally Morley says, "When my husband got here and saw the services in our churches, the first thing he bought himself was a tambourine."[66] One can hear the same type of music in the Pentecostal churches that one hears on the popular radio programs or in the corner *cantinas,* but the words have been changed to tell of God's love and wonder-working power. When the instruments start playing and a trio of national Christions begins to sing a hymn in *pasillo* rhythm, the atmosphere is definitely Colombian.

One of my more interesting interviews with Pentecostal members was with Manuel Bernal, the choir leader and a musician in the church in Bucaramanga. Besides singing any of the four parts, he plays the piano, organ, accordion, and some on the bass viol. He expressed some of his philosophy on the use of music in the churches:

> Personally I don't use the *pasillo,* but am not against it because it is an indigenous form of music of the people. The kind of music to be used depends on the place and the people. In some places a choir with classical music would fail, but a *ranchera* would do well. God can use a *pasillo* to touch the hearts of the people. . . . We should use the music that will attract them and speak to them the most. I see no difference in using a *pasillo* or *bambuco.* The important thing is the message.[67]

The Pentecostals also make full use of the *serenata,* a long-established custom of Spanish and Latin American people. But instead of a lover singing love songs to his beloved near her window in the early hours of the morning, groups of Pentecostal musicians and singers move from house to house singing of the love of God and His invitation to sinful men. Most of the Pentecostal pastors I interviewed gave the use of the *serenata* as a definite factor in their growth.

> One of the most fruitful methods my church has used to win new people is the *serenata.* We have several trios that do this and a number of families have been won in this way. When one man—a sorcerer—heard a *serenata* he was moved to tears. Later he attended our services, was converted, and burned all his books on witchcraft and sorcery.[68]

Domingo Zuniga sums up what he considers to be four main

factors in the growth of the United Pentecostal Church in Colombia: (1) "Every member of the Colombian church is an evangelist"; (2) zeal for the basic Jesus Only doctrine: repentance and faith in Christ, baptism in water "in the name," and Holy Spirit baptism; (3) the ministry and leadership of the Colombian pastors and leaders; and (4) the fact that "our church satisfies the hunger and thirst of the people more than other churches do."[69]

OVER-ALL FACTORS

In the interviews with pastors and denominational leaders, I asked which factors the informants felt were most important in the growth of the Pentecostal churches. Fourteen denominational leaders and twenty-eight pastors, from both Pentecostal and non-Pentecostal churches, were included in this

TABLE 11

MAJOR FACTORS IN PENTECOSTAL CHURCH GROWTH

FACTORS	MENTIONED BY PENTECOSTALS	MENTIONED BY NON-PENTECOSTALS
1. Enthusiasm and activity of the members	15	21
2. Emotionalism that appeals to the masses	2	21
3. Emphasis on healing and miracles	4	12
4. Apprenticeship system of training leaders	3	9
5. Emphasis on the Holy Spirit and prayer	8	8
6. Emphasis on church planting	14	2
7. Self-support system of the churches	5	4
8. Opportunity given to all to participate	0	8
9. Their indoctrination system for new believers	4	1
10. Their proselytizing activities	0	5

sampling. Other factors not listed in the following table were also given, but were mentioned so few times that they are not included here.

The factor mentioned most often by both Pentecostal and non-Pentecostal pastors and leaders was the enthusiasm and activity of the Pentecostal church members. This would have to do primarily with personal evangelism and outreach efforts. The other factors given most often by Pentecostal pastors and leaders were: the emphasis on church planting, the emphasis on the Holy Spirit and prayer, and the self-support system of the churches.

The non-Pentecostal leaders considered a principal factor in Pentecostal growth to be its emotionalism, which appeals to the Latin American temperament. This would have to do primarily with the kind of meetings and campaigns that they conduct. Following this, and the activity of the members, other factors considered most important by non-Pentecostal leaders were: the emphasis on healing and miracles, the apprenticeship system of training leaders, the emphasis on the Holy Spirit and prayer, and the opportunity given to all to participate in some way in the meetings.

In the previous analysis of the four leading Pentecostal denominations in Colombia, we have attempted to pinpoint the outstanding or unique factors in growth in the case of each of these churches. It is apparent that certain factors that have already been mentioned in the case of one of these denominations, are applicable to all the Pentecostal churches we have considered, and may be termed overall factors in their growth. Then there are other important reasons for their growth which we have not really dealt with as yet. In this part of the chapter we will wrap up these major overall factors in growth which are present in all the Pentecostal denominations that we are considering, howbeit in varying degrees.

To start with, the Pentecostals have what might be termed a built-in advantage for church growth, because of the appeal of their message and meetings to the popular classes of Colombia. This brings us to the first two factors, which are largely sociological.

APPEAL OF THE PENTECOSTAL MESSAGE OF DIVINE HEALING

Pentecostals are convinced that divine healing is for all who will believe, and that it is one of the principal means of bringing new people to Christ.

> The doctrine of divine healing has always been emphasized with Pentecostal churches. . . . These men felt that "even a casual study of the New Testament makes it clear that divine healing was the chief cause for which Christ received the attention of the nation of His day.
>
> Furthermore, they reasoned, the Great Commission that Christ gave to the Church included the command to heal the sick. Likewise, they were convinced that "the healing revival is the God appointed means to reach the unsaved masses in the heathen lands, or where Protestant Christianity has a feeble hold."[70]
>
> The cornerstone of "deliverance evangelism," as it was referred to among Pentecostals, is the belief that just as God wants everyone to be saved from sin, so also does He desire everyone to be well. The task of deliverance evangelists, therefore, is to proclaim this truth and to encourage their listeners to believe it.[71]

To the question, What place does divine healing have in winning new people to the church?, most of the Pentecostal pastors interviewed answered that it is "one of the best baits there are to attract new people."[72] A United Pentecostal pastor said, "The object of healing for the unsaved is as a bait. It attracts their attention to the power of Christ, who can also save."[73] A pastor of the Assemblies of God expressed that the promise of divine healing has "great attraction. Many come to our services just for this."[74] Speaking of the importance of healing in an evangelistic campaign, another Assemblies of God pastor said, "It is very important in a campaign because the people want to see miracles. When there are healings, the people talk about it and bring others. Everyone says, 'Let's go to

the campaign.' "[75] A United Pentecostal announcement illustrates the appeal:

> Attention! The United Pentecostal Church of Colombia
> . . . invites you . . . to hear the Word of God with preachers
> and trios anointed with the Holy Spirit. Bring your sick and
> Jesus Christ will heal them, for He said, "I will go and heal
> them" (Mt 8:7).[76]

I attended an Assemblies of God campaign in Pereira when
the church there was very young. At the beginning of the
service, the pastor asked the believers, "How many here tonight
have received divine healing?" Many raised their hands. He
then said, "Those who believe God can heal here tonight, say
amen." Many responded. The message itself illustrates the
twofold Pentecostal emphasis on salvation and healing.

> Sin has two aspects—spiritual and physical. Christ healed
> spiritually and physically; I repeat: spiritually *and* physically.
> We have come to Pereira not just with a gospel of words, but
> also of demonstrations. . . . Christ saves and heals today just
> as He did then. He died to save; He lives to heal. At the be-
> ginning of this service, many raised their hands testifying that
> they had been healed. How many of you would like to re-
> ceive salvation or healing tonight? Come forward.[77]

A number of people made their way to the front of the make-
shift platform, and the pastor continued:

> Those of you who have come forward for healing, come
> here in front of me and I am going to pray for you. Those
> who want to accept Christ, pass to the room at the side and
> counsellors will help you. . . . Now we are going to pray, and
> you will see with your own eyes God's healing in these per-
> sons. A woman came to me today, saying, "I have heard that
> in this church there is healing." She had a foot completely
> without feeling. We prayed and God healed her.[78]

While the rest of the visitors and believers looked on, each
one that had gone forward for healing was then asked what
sickness or ailment needed healing. As the pastor raised his
hand over each person and prayed, the members of the church

were crying out for God to work in a supernatural way. The emotion in the service rose to its peak in this, its spectacular moment, as all prayed at once for God to heal. After a few minutes, the fervor died down, and the service was ended. Some likely went away doubting, but others very impressed. To me, this service, as well as other healing campaigns that I have witnessed, had some of the atmosphere of a circus side-show, but there is no getting around the fact that they appeal a great deal to many of the people in Colombia.

It is significant to consider the effect of the religious and cultural background of the people on their way of thinking. Roman Catholicism in this country has emphasized miracle and mystery, and these have always appealed greatly to the masses. I have personally watched as devout Roman Catholics have visited the famous statue of the "miraculous Christ" in one of the Catholic churches in the city of Buga. One person after another approached this "Christ," kneeled before it, and wiped a piece of cloth or cotton on the part of the statue painted as blood stains. The people believe that by then wiping the piece of cloth or cotton on the afflicted part of a sick person's body, that person can be healed. One has only to see the faces of these simple and devout people as they kneel before the "Christ" to realize that there is a great deal of hope and faith in this miraculous way of healing. And it is in this context that Pentecostalism also emphasizes miracle (i.e., divine healing) and mystery (i.e., speaking in unknown tongues, prophesying concerning the future). And it is because of this background that the gospel of healing has special relevance and appeal in Latin America.

> There is such a preoccupation with psychosomatic disease, especially the "evil eye" and the "susto," "fright or shock." . . . Even in Roman Catholicism much of the focus of attention upon the saints is related to healing, and it is not strange that this same concern should carry over into these Protestant communities.[79]

I can understand this, for on a couple of occasions, Colombians have come to me to be cured because someone gave them the "evil eye." They understood that as an evangelical minister, I had the power to free them from the influence of the evil spell which they believed had been placed upon them. I have also found, even among those who have been believers in our churches for many years, that there are a great deal of superstitious beliefs associated with their ailments and afflictions.

To people with this background, who neither understand sickness nor can afford to go to medical doctors, the Pentecostal offer of immediate and miraculous healing has tremendous appeal.

APPEAL OF PENTECOSTAL MEETINGS, ESPECIALLY TO THE
    LOWER CLASSES

What are the characteristics of Pentecostal meetings that appeal to the common people?

An atmosphere of joy and fiesta. It has already been pointed out that the factor in Pentecostal growth most often mentioned by the non-Pentecostal pastors and leaders, is the appeal that the emotional and the spectacular in Pentecostalism have to the Latin American temperament. Dr. George Biddulph sums up this opinion when he says, "There is an emotionalism in Pentecostal churches that satisfies the Latin temperament."[80] In chapter 4, we mentioned that one of the distinctives of Pentecostalism is the intense emotional character of its meetings. Obviously this type of meeting appeals more to many Colombians than the rather staid and structured services that are common in many of the non-Pentecostal churches. Ray Zuercher, of the Gospel Missionary Union, adds that "this emotional content meets a need, especially in the lower classes."[81] Dr. Alan Neely agrees: "The spontaneity and enthusiasm in the services are attractive to the lower clases, especially the marginal people who are looking for something to identify with."[82]

Life for Colombians of the poorer classes is usually hard, routine, and monotonous, with very little excitement or diversion. Pentecostal meetings offer a real change from the drabness of daily life—joy, emotion, and a sense of exhilaration.

Rev. Ralph Hines, missionary field leader of WEC, says, "One of the main factors in Pentecostal growth is the enthusiasm in their services in preaching, singing, and participating."[83] The result is that "these people, with so many problems and a life of hardships, find release and joy."[84] In asking the Pentecostal members themselves why they like their church better than others, one woman replied, "There is more life, power, enthusiasm, and activity than in other churches." A woman from a Panamerican church, in comparing her church with others, said,

> You don't feel the warmth, the fellowship, the power, the liberty, as in my church. There is much order and many lovely things about services in other churches, but one doesn't feel. . . .[85]

I asked some of the Pentecostal pastors why former members of other evangelical churches had later joined their churches. One United Pentecostal pastor replied, "In the Pentecostal church one feels something he doesn't feel in other churches, something supernatural, ecstasy, joy."[86] Octavio Moreno, the pastor of the largest Assemblies of God church in Bogota, said, "They feel more life, enthusiasm, and activity in our church."[87]

In contrast, our services in the non-Pentecostal churches often seem to fail to appeal. One leader expressed that "our meetings are often without color—unattractive, uninteresting, monotonous."[88] Whether one agrees with this, apparently a lot of Colombians that are going to the Pentecostal churches feel this way.

In attending a number of Pentecostal meetings myself, I have often felt that the Pentecostal service provides a substitute for what many of these people found in their fiestas before they were converted. I attended just such a fiesta in First United Pentecostal a Jesus Only church, in Palmira. When I arrived at their "temple" that Sunday morning, a stream of people was entering that would have delighted the pastor of any of the other churches in the city. The ladies came with their long black hair, starched dresses, and white shoes. Some of the men wore suits, but one could tell that most of them were poor.

The pastor, Jesus Cardozo, spoke with much enthusiasm and spirit, and had the people right in his hands:

> The Lord Jesus was the Lord of miracles—right? He changed the water into wine—right? Amen! He raised from the dead the son of the nobleman—hallelujah to the Lord! He raised Lazarus from the dead before the eyes of His followers! Glory to God! Jesus is the same today! Amen! He can work the same miracles today! Amen! Oh, that we can believe *one thing* today—that Jesus is the same yesterday, today, and forever! Amen! Hallelujah! Hallelujah!
>
> Now let's pray, and pray in faith, with the authority of the Word of God and the power of the Holy Spirit, in the name of Jesus![89]

At this point everyone is standing. The pastor is shouting his prayer, and the people are all praying at once. It begins as a dull roar that grows to a crescendo of noise. Some are clapping, others are looking up with arms outstretched, shaking their hands in the air, and concentrating in prayer.

This is the climax! The whole sermon, delivery, and invitation have led to this grand finale. The pastor prays for the healing of the sick. The whole congregation is in prayer, and the man directing the service begins to speak in tongues. Elderly ladies are lifting their arms in prayer and ecstasy. Some men are shouting. The whole atmosphere is charged with emotion and expectancy.

Finally the praying and action begin to calm down. Believers, happy and revived in spirit, begin to sing and clap to the accompaniment of an electric guitar, "I sing glory to God; my soul He set free; glory to God." The platform leader asks for a unanimous "Glory to God." All shout "GLORY TO GOD!", raise their hands, and clap in unison. It has all been a very exciting experience for them, a Pentecostal fiesta that has thrilled their beings in the drabness of their daily lives.

> If I were a humble, poor person, whose life was a day-to-day struggle, I could go to the church and just praise the

Lord, rejoice, participate, and forget about the bitterness of daily life.[90]

The opportunity to participate. An example of this is a service I attended at the Assemblies of God Bethel Church in Bogota. Between those who led in prayer, Bible reading, congregational singing, special numbers, reports and announcements, testimonies, and the message itself, at least twenty people took part in the service.

Ed Murphy stressed this as well. He and other Overseas Crusades leaders had been in Bogota for a conference of Panamerican church leaders. In one service they counted sixty-five believers who participated on the platform. Some played instruments—guitars, *tiples,* accordions, tambourines, piano, harmonica, and bass drum. There were solos, duets, trios, and quartets. Others led in prayer, Bible-reading, choruses, testimonies, the collection of the offering, hymns, and the message itself. Murphy emphasized what an interesting and stimulating service it had been for him and for those that were present.[91]

I can remember attending and observing a Pentecostal service in a city where there are also a number of non-Pentecostal churches. There had been a lot of participation on the platform and by the congregation that morning, and the service certainly did not drag. After the meeting closed, I went to a non-Pentecostal church and caught part of the service there. It was a one-man show, as the pastor droned on and on. The congregation was passive, bored, and restless to get the service over with and leave. So was I.

Of course not everyone can be on the platform. But in the Pentecostal churches, everyone still has the sensation of direct participation in being able to pray aloud with the whole congregation, interject amens and hallelujahs during the sermon, clap during the singing, or speak in tongues, and usually with almost complete liberty. As one Pentecostal pastor said, "In our services there is liberty for praise and worship as the Holy Spirit leads each one to express himself. Everyone can participate."[92]

As against the "spectator religion" so prevalent in mainline Protestantism, the Pentecostals really participate in their services. Almost anyone, singly or with a group, is welcome to stand forth and "sing a special"; there is testimony, the calling out of requests at the time for prayer, the vocal joining in prayer together, hand clapping, and shouting. And in the "Amen! . . . Hallelujah! . . . Thank you, Jesus! . . . Praise the Lord! . . ." there is definite pattern, a litany of worship by the participating congregation.[93]

Incorporation of indigenous aspects of the culture. In their music, atmosphere, and preaching, the Pentecostal services are very indigenous. We have already mentioned that the "Jesus Only" people utilize the popular rhythms and instruments of Colombia in their music. *Tiples,* guitars, tambourines, bongos, and other instruments accompany songs set to the rhythm of *pasillos, danzas,* and boleros.

Because the Panamerican and United Pentecostal Churches are indigenous and Colombian, they can simply do things in their services that seem right to them as Colombians. We mentioned a Panamerican meeting where sixty-five different people took part. If missionaries would have had their hand in this, it is unlikely the service would have followed the course it did.

Drama is loved by Colombians, and drama is used in Pentecostal preaching. The emphasis is less on a logical and profound presentation of doctrinal truth, and more on God's supernatural power and His working in and through Bible personalities. And as we have seen in parts of Pentecostal messages already quoted in this chapter, the preacher aims at congregational association with the Bible personalities, and appropriation of their victories. In other words, the congregation enters into the drama which is presented through Bible personalities and stories.

A sense of "feeling" the presence of God. Pentecostals enjoy their meetings because they "feel" God's presence and His working in their midst in a special and supernatural way. When they leave their meetings, they feel they can really say from personal experience, "We have been with the Lord."

One question that I asked both Pentecostal and non-Pentecostal members was, What do you like most about your own local church? Each member was asked to pick three of the following six possibilities: (1) the doctrine; (2) the marvelous personal experiences through the Holy Spirit; (3) the opportunity to serve and participate; (4) the feeling of warmth and fellowship in the church; (5) the pastor and his preaching; and (6) the standards the church holds.

The answer which rated highest and was chosen most often by the Pentecostals was, the marvelous personal experiences through the Holy Spirit. This answer rated very low for the non-Pentecostal members interviewed, for whom doctrine rated the highest. I do not think this means, however, that the non-Pentecostals would not like to have a more personal and vital experience of communication with God in their services. I just do not think they could choose this answer because they had not experienced this very much in their own church services, which emphasize one man (the pastor) giving a study (lecture) on the Bible and doctrine. For Latin Americans, whose background is Roman Catholic and whose temperament is more emotional than ours, it seems to be very important to "feel" God's presence and working. And this personal experience of "feeling" God and sensing His presence is what they find in the Pentecostal churches.

> Pentecostals . . . have a highly significant system of communication. In place of the Latin which only the priests understand, Pentecostals may all receive the gift of tongues— an even more ecstatic experience than reciting the memorized phrases of a dead language. . . . These people do not have the miraculous wafer to offer the people, but they can offer the promise of miraculous healing, not only as the gift of God but as a proof of a measure of faith and of the fact that God has answered the people's communication to Him. . . . Despite certain excesses which may characterize some of these Pentecostal movements . . . one must, however, recognize the fact that . . . people experience a sense of communication, of worship, and of the divine-human encounter.[94]

So the Pentecostal meetings and their message of divine healing have great appeal to many Colombians, and constitute important factors in their growth. But the Pentecostals have not stopped with this advantage. They have built upon it some objectives, strategy, and methods which have proven very effective in producing church growth.

CLEAR OBJECTIVE OF BUILDING INDIGENOUS LOCAL CHURCHES

Usually people and organizations achieve what they aim for, and this is true in missions as well. If the emphasis is on institutions and secondary ministries, then these will generally develop and prosper more than the churches. If a denomination's emphasis is on education, the greater results will be seen in its schools and students. But if the emphasis of a denomination is on planting and building up local churches, the result will more likely be growing churches that reproduce themselves.

In chapter 2, we compared the ministries and institutions of the different denominations in this study. The Pentecostals are way ahead in multiplying local churches and members, but they have far less institutions and secondary ministries than the other Protestant churches. In contrast, a strong emphasis of the Presbyterians has been education, and the United Presbyterian Church has more teachers and students than pastors and church members. In general, the faith missions have the widest variety of institutions and secondary ministries, and from my own observation, some of these operate almost independently of the local churches.

The Pentecostal churches, on the other hand, dedicate the great majority of their time, personnel, and money to planting and building up local churches. Evangelistic and healing campaigns, as in the case of the Assemblies of God, are directly tied to planting churches. Specialized ministries, such as radio, are usually sponsored by local churches. And where they have Bible institutes, these are set up, not as separate entities, but as an arm of the church for growth and expansion.

Not only this, but existing churches are organized for church planting; they are, in Ed Murphy's words, "mission agencies."[95]

The Assemblies of God concentrates on the *campo blanco* system, the Foursquare church on branch Sunday schools, the Panamerican Mission on home Bible-study groups and out-stations, and the United Pentecostal Church on preaching points. But by whatever name these outreach points are called, the goal is the same: to multiply local churches. Glen Kramer of the Assemblies of God summarizes this emphasis:

> Our *principal goal always* is to evangelize and establish churches. We are local-church centered. Some denominations have their emphasis on education and other ministries; our emphasis is on local churches.[96]

The Pentecostal churches are also self-supporting. Both the United Pentecostal and Panamerican churches receive practically no outside financial help or subsidy. Yet these churches are growing and multiplying, building new church buildings, opening new works, and in the case of the United Pentecostal Church, even sending and supporting national missionaries in other countries.

The Assemblies of God likewise believes in a self-supporting Colombian church, and this is clearly stated in the constitution of the national church:

> The General Council recognizes as one of the basic principles of the Church its duty (a) to be self-propagating, (b) to be self-governing through its officials, pastors, and deacons, (c) to be self-supporting financially. The missionaries have been sent with the purpose of helping to evangelize the country and establish the National Church. The General Council takes the responsibility for the support of these missionaries and will also cooperate with national efforts to establish institutes and centers of evangelization that are not within the financial capability of the National Church, . . . but it does not accept the responsibility for the support of pastors of the local churches since this does not pertain to its sphere of effort.[97]

One of the reasons that Assemblies of God leaders give for their growth is "the unapologetic teaching in regard to tithing and

the insistence that each church and congregation economically
support its own work."[98]

The United Pentecostal Church began its work in Colombia
in the larger cities—Bucaramanga, Barranquilla, and Cali.
Later it entered cities such as Bogota, Medellin, and Pereira.
These cities became centers for planting churches in the innumerable *barrios* and in surrounding towns and villages. This
is not to say that their rural work is not strong, but it did not
receive priority. The larger cities were the initial targets for
establishing churches, and these city churches have then evan-
gelized and planted churches in the surrounding rural areas.
For example, the Cali church gave birth to the Palmira church,
and to numerous other churches in the *Departamentos* of the
Valle and Caldas. The Pereira churches have also opened new
works in the whole surrounding rural area.

The Panamerican Mission began its first church in Bogota.
Then other churches were started in Pereira and Medellin. Recently, Cali has become a target center. And as in the case of
Pereira, the city churches then send their leaders to open new
works in the neighboring villages and towns.

The Foursquare church has placed priority on establishing
strong churches in cities in the northern part of Colombia—
Barrancabermeja, Barranquilla, Bucaramanga, and Cucuta.

The Assemblies of God is the only Pentecostal church in our
study that began its work in Colombia in a rural setting—
Sogamoso. And it is significant that they really did not experience rapid church growth until they centered their efforts in
Bogota, the largest city in the country. Other strategic centers
for the Assemblies of God are now the cities of Cali, in the
southwestern part of the country; Medellin, in the west-central
area; and Barranquilla and Cartagena, in the north. From
these larger cities, their work has spread to smaller cities such
as Pereira and Palmira, and from these cities to the surrounding
rural areas.

Lewis Morley of the United Pentecostal Church expressed this city-centered strategy:

> It has been my policy never to concentrate in the country, but in the cities. We should go where the majority of the people are, and then let them go out. Country people can't evangelize the city people, but city people can evangelize the country people. We take care not to put a country person in a city church, nor a city pastor in a country church. They just don't jive.[99]

Some of the rest of us in other Protestant missions have lacked this common-sense approach to missions strategy.

IMMEDIATE FOLLOW-UP AND INCORPORATION OF NEW CONVERTS

Pentecostals are very zealous about winning new people to their faith. And when they have won someone, they are equally zealous about leading that person into baptism and church membership, the charismatic experiences, and service for Christ and the local church. I have personally observed again and again, how a new Pentecostal convert will be visited, encouraged, invited to church, and sometimes almost "surrounded" by the brethren, so that he will not forget what has happened in his life or go back on his decision. Of course many do go back, but generally not for lack of follow-up.

Most of the interviews pointed to another difference, in the fact that Pentecostal pastors make every effort to enroll the new convert *immediately* in an indoctrination class—if possible within a week. This does not give the new convert time to forget what he has done, and it begins to fortify him in his new faith almost immediately. Once a person is enrolled in an indoctrination class, there is much less likelihood of his falling away again.

The Assemblies of God churches place much emphasis on the *Reglamento Local,* a standard booklet containing a series of studies for new converts to prepare them for baptism and membership. It deals with the main doctrines of the Assemblies of God, the privileges and responsibilities of members, local

church organization, and special ceremonies, such as marriage
and the dedication of children. It is really quite a complete and
practical booklet for indoctrinating new converts and preparing
them for membership.

> The *Reglamento Local* helps in that it mirrors our philos-
> ophy of doctrine, church administration, and the *campo
> blanco* system, so that from the beginning, the new Christian
> is imbued and oriented in this philosophy.[100]

The United Pentecostal Church, while zealous about follow-
up, does not have as definite a plan or material for the instruction and indoctrination of new believers as does the Assemblies
of God; in fact, this is one of the greatest weaknesses of this
denomination. It is also the only church that baptizes new converts within a week of their conversion. But while they are
weak in indoctrination, new believers are not allowed to grow
cold; they are immediately encouraged to seek the baptism of
the Holy Spirit, and to begin witnessing, praying, and participating in the life and activities of the local church. The United
Pentecostal Church places four primary objectives before each
new convert: (1) "Don't change your faith—you are now a
Pentecostal"; (2) "Don't forsake your church—attend constantly"; (3) "Be baptized in the name of the Lord Jesus and
then seek the experience of Holy Spirit baptism—do it right
away"; (4) "Witness to others."[101]

INVOLVEMENT OF THE MEMBERS IN EVANGELISM AND
    OUTREACH

Ignacio Guevara, of the Panamerican Mission, says,

> One of the main reasons for our growth is the mobilization
> of the church. Every pastor ought to mobilize the believers,
> if possible one-hundred percent, in evangelization, in visita-
> tion, and in home Bible studies. They are the ones that win
> souls. The pastor perfects the brethren, but they are the ones
> that go and win souls.[102]

All the Pentecostal denominations stress the necessity of
every believer giving continual testimony of his faith to others,

both in spontaneous daily witness and in organized church efforts in evangelism through visitation, open-air meetings, and other methods of outreach.

We have already seen some of the extent to which the Pentecostals are achieving this. The Foursquare church has the mobilization of all believers in evangelism as one of its major and constant goals. The United Pentecostal Church expects every member to be an aggressive evangelist, and the amount of evangelistic activity carried on by its members is certainly exceptional. Aldemar Pardo, of the Bible Societies in Colombia, speaking of the Jesus Only people, says,

> These people are more *Penzotti* [a system of door-to-door outreach of the Bible Societies] than we are. They witness everywhere—on the busses, in the schools, in their neighborhoods—wherever they go.[103]

Evidence of the Pentecostal membership activity can be seen in the fact that almost all the non-Pentecostal pastors and leaders interviewed recognized this as one of the major factors in their growth. A Baptist pastor praised "their boldness and determination in witnessing and serving," and added: "These people just have no laziness about them. The pastor says, 'Let's go and do this,' and they do it."[104]

> They believe in making disciples of their people, instead of "just believers." There is a strong emphasis on the responsibility of each believer as a consecrated witness. . . . They have very few loafers.[105]

It is this constant activity of the Pentecostal members that prompted the authors of *Church Growth in Latin America* to write:

> The Pentecostal system leads to involvement and self-propagation. The Pentecostals work to involve all their members in the various aspects of their work in a vital grass-roots system of witness and evangelism. By means of open-air services, by myriad preaching points and congregations, the Pentecostals approach a near total level of lay participation.[106]

AN EFFECTIVE APPRENTICESHIP SYSTEM

Dr. Alan Neely gives as one of the main factors in Pentecostal growth "their whole system of theological education and the use of laymen as leaders and pastors."[107] Every Pentecostal denomination we have mentioned has one or more definite methods for planting new churches. But none of these churches has enough full-time paid pastors to begin to attend all the *campos blancos,* preaching points, or branch Sunday schools that have been opened. So the Pentecostals, more than any others, motivate and delegate responsibility to lay leaders to direct these efforts. Every local church is expected to be a recruitment agency for this source of personnel, and is able to multiply its outreach many times over through its lay leaders.

But this is just the first step. We have seen how all pastors in the Pentecostal churches get their start as lay leaders in local churches, and there must show definite potential for leadership and soul-winning. Only then may they go on to direct a new outreach effort or incipient church. And only if they are successful in building up a congregation do they go on to become pastors. This whole apprenticeship system has a built-in screening process which tends to eliminate much professionalism in the ministry, and allows only those with the necessary gifts and leadership to become pastors. Leaders rise to the level of their vision, activity, spiritual gifts, and leadership competence. Success in the ministry itself—in winning people to the faith and in building up local churches—is the real requirement for advancement in this system. No amount of education or talent will substitute for this practical requirement.

> Pentecostals develop pastoral leaders from among the laity. They depend on God's effectual call. Leaders emerge from among the converts through in-service training at the level of the local congregation. Here pastoral and spiritual gifts and personal consecration are tested and developed. Calling to the ministry is verified by success in communicating the faith and multiplying churches. Finally ministers are accepted or rejected by the approval or disapproval of the members of the church.[108]

The Assemblies of God and Foursquare churches have Bible institutes which give formal theological training, but these institutes do not bypass this essential apprenticeship system; they work with it and through it in the preparation given. Only proven leaders may enroll in the Assemblies of God Bible institute in the first place, and in the institute's preparation, as much emphasis is given to practical experience as to academic achievement.

> The Bible institute training program is set up to fit the needs of the churches and *campos blancos,* and the situation of the pastors and leaders. Students must be proven before they are admitted to the Bible institute. This is biblical.
>
> At the same time, the Assemblies of God adapts its institute to the men who are preparing and to the situation of the churches. For example, a man who is a pastor has a wife and family and directs a church outside of Bogota. He goes to the Institute on a Monday, begins classes on Tuesday, continues through that week and the next until the Friday of the second week, then goes back to his church. So he is gone from his church every other Sunday. Laymen take his place when he is gone. Everything about the institute is related to the worker and pastor and to their churches in a practical way.[109]

EMPHASIS ON THE HOLY SPIRIT AND PRAYER

There is no getting around the fact that the Pentecostal churches are revived churches. By "revived," I mean that the majority of the members (1) live separated and godly lives; (2) pray a great deal, at least in the church; (3) trust implicitly in God to work in and through them; (4) are very enthusiastic about witnessing to others about their faith; (5) are faithful and active in their local churches; and (6) are generous givers. It is one thing to have good methods and objectives in our churches; it is another to have people who are willing and enthusiastic about carrying them out. We have mentioned that in the Pentecostal churches, lay leaders are used a great deal, and that the members are mobilized in evangelistic outreach efforts. But if the lay leaders and members were not willing and enthusiastic about serving, the methods of outreach and evangelism would not work. A very important factor in creating this willingness, enthusiasm, and spirit of revival in the Pentecostal believers and churches, is their emphasis on the Holy Spirit and prayer in their lives.

In Pentecostal churches, every believer is not only to seek the baptism of the Holy Spirit, but also the continual filling and power of the Spirit for service. "There is emphasis on the power of the Holy Spirit in the believer to overcome and to witness. There is also an emphasis on the gifts of the Holy Spirit in the believer for service."[110] Eugene Kelly, director of the Christian and Missionary Alliance in Colombia, mentions the average Pentecostal's "implicit faith that God will work through him through the power of the Holy Spirit."[111] The Pentecostal's attitude is one of "God and I can do great things together." This is clearly reflected in the words of one Pentecostal pastor, "Any man, any woman, any person can do miracles with the power of the Holy Spirit. Every believer can work miracles because every believer can have the power of the Holy Spirit."[112] The importance of the power of the Holy Spirit for witnessing is continually emphasized by Pentecostal preachers:

> But you say, "I'm afraid to witness; I don't have enough courage." Then the Lord has already given the answer to your need in Acts 1:8—the power of the Holy Spirit to witness in your neighborhood, in your city, in neighboring towns, in the nation, and even to the uttermost part of the world.[113]

Concerning the gifts of the Holy Spirit for service, Ed Murphy comments regarding the Panamerican Mission:

> They have a healthy emphasis on the Holy Spirit. They have moved from an extreme position on the charismatic gifts, on the one hand, and they have put emphasis on the gifts of the Holy Spirit which are given for service and administration. When we teach in this group on discovering and using the gifts the Holy Spirit has given us, this is no new thing to them.[114]

Dr. George Biddulph of the Interamerican Mission admits that "the Holy Spirit is working in the Pentecostal Churches. They have put emphasis on the gifts of the Holy Spirit and their use and expression. This emphasis has been lacking in the more formal denominations."[115]

Pentecostal churches also emphasize and practice prayer more than the other Protestant denominations do. Most of the Pentecostal leaders and pastors interviewed consider the continual practice of prayer and fasting to be a principal factor in their growth. While traditional denominations often have difficulty getting a majority of their members to attend a prayer meeting once a week, Pentecostals seem to relish attending several prayer services a week. Besides having regular mid-week prayer meetings, most Pentecostal churches have all-night "prayer vigils," and many have daily prayer meetings either in the early morning or evening. For example, the United Pentecostal church in the *barrio* of Cuba in Pereira has a prayer meeting every morning at 5:00 A.M. with a good attendance. Every two weeks there is a complete day of prayer and fasting. The Assemblies of God church in the *barrio* of Bello Horizonte in Bogota also has a daily prayer meeting at 5:00 A.M., as well as an open-ended prayer meeting on Friday nights.

> There we meet to pray and fast for the work. It is a time of confession, heart-searching, and testimony, but especially of prayer. . . . We must have power before we can go and minister to others. I get them to forget about themselves and pray for the lost. We must put this first.[116]

In the questionnaire for members, I asked which was the favorite meeting of the week as far as the informants were concerned. For the majority of Pentecostals interviewed, it was prayer meeting; for non-Pentecostals, Sunday school. We praise God for the interest our people have in studying the Bible, but somehow they do not seem to enjoy or feel the need of praying the way the Pentecostals do.

Pentecostals are aware that they place more emphasis on the Holy Spirit and prayer than most protestant denominations do, and largely because of this, most of them feel that their church is more spiritual than other Protestant churches. To the question, Do you feel that your church is more spiritual than the others in the city?, the majority—forty-two out of fifty-two—replied yes. One Pentecostal member expressed why she felt this way: "We walk in more holiness and study the Bible more. There is more spirituality, more prayer, and more of the Spirit."[117] Another said, "There is more desire to pray, more desire to work and serve the Lord, and more love between the brethren."[118] Many of the non-Pentecostal pastors and leaders recognize the greater emphasis and practice of prayer by the Pentecostals. One of them, a Gospel Missionary Union pastor, frankly admits, "They *do* pray more; they *do* seek the Lord more; and they *do* witness more."[119]

SUMMARY

To close this chapter, I repeat the eight principal overall factors in the growth of the Pentecostal churches in Colombia:

1. Appeal of the Pentecostal message of divine healing.
2. Appeal of Pentecostal meetings, especially to the lower classes
3. Clear objective of building indigenous local churches
4. Strategy of placing priority on larger cities as centers for church-planting efforts
5. Immediate follow-up and incorporation of new converts into the life and activities of the church
6. Enthusiastic involvement of a high percentage of the members in personal evangelism and church outreach efforts
7. A practical and effective apprenticeship system of training lay leaders and pastors
8. Emphasis on the Holy Spirit and prayer in the life of every believer and congregation

6

Evaluation and Conclusions

Strong church growth is possible in Colombia, as the Pentecostals especially have proven. In the previous chapter, we considered the major factors in their exceptional growth; in this concluding chapter, we will point out some of the dangers and negative aspects in the Pentecostal movement in Colombia, as well as the major lessons that we can learn from it.

We need to remember that while in the overall picture the Pentecostal denominations have had the greatest church growth, not all of the Pentecostal local churches have done well. The Assemblies of God church in Pereira has not prospered particularly, and some of their churches in Bogota have grown very slowly. There are Panamerican and United Pentecostal churches that have had problems and difficulties, and have stagnated. Then, on the other hand, there are non-Pentecostal local churches that have found the way to exceptional church growth. The CMA church in Neiva has been a model for church growth. The GMU has multiplied its churches and has experienced good growth in the city of Cali and in the Caldas region. The Southern Baptists constitute the largest Trinitarian Protestant denomination in Colombia, except for the Seventh-Day Adventists. And the Interamerican Mission and the Worldwide Evangelization Crusade have had good growth, though not as great as that of the Pentecostals. Much could be learned about church growth from a study of the exceptional churches within these denominations as well.

WEAKNESSES

We also need to recognize that in the Pentecostal churches and their growth, there are negative aspects that we are not anxious to follow. The fact that the United Pentecostal Church is winning so many Colombians to its faith would be considered a great victory and blessing by all the Evangelicals in Colombia, if it were not for the fact that this church holds to and teaches certain doctrines which we believe are far from the truth, especially concerning the Godhead and the doctrine of salvation. It also concerns us to see many Pentecostals who depend so much on feelings and emotions, and often have very little depth of understanding of the Word of God. One of the things that stood out so sharply in many of my interviews with Pentecostal members, but especially with those of the Jesus Only churches, was the little factual knowledge of Bible content that they had.

In the questionnaires for non-Pentecostal pastors and denominational leaders, I included a supplement in which I asked their opinions regarding the Pentecostal churches and their growth. One of the questions was, What are your main criticisms of the Pentecostal churches, and what do you consider to be their main weaknesses? The five answers given most often were: (1) doctrinal excesses and emotional extremes; (2) their proselytizing efforts; (3) the exclusivistic attitude of "We have more of the Spirit than you have"; (4) the lack of adequate indoctrination, which leads to instability in the believers; and (5) their ability to reach only the people of the lower classes. Other criticisms mentioned less often were: (6) the antiintellectual attitude that many of them have; (7) their lack of involvement in social problems; (8) the lack of theological training of many of the pastors and leaders; (9) the dangers inherent in the *caudillo* system that prevails in many of the Pentecostal denominations and churches; and (10) the tendency to divisions in their churches. Generally the greatest amount of criticism was leveled at the United Pentecostal Church, and the least at the Assemblies of God.

LACK OF THEOLOGICAL PREPARATION

There is, I believe, a correlation between numbers 1, 4, 5, 6, 8, and 10 above. Doctrinal excesses, the lack of adequate indoctrination in many of the churches, the ability to reach only the lower classes, and the tendency to divisions within these churches and denominations (again, due in part to the lack of a firm theological base), begin in large part because of "the lack of theological training of many of the pastors and leaders." Scholastic attainment and theological preparation do not count for much in many of the Pentecostal churches. If one is successful in proselytizing and has the charismatic gifts, a strong personality, and the ability to lead, he can often become a pastor. God's hand and seal of anointing are upon him. Even if he should preach and confuse the ark of Noah with the ark of the covenant—no matter—he is God's man. Theological knowledge and a thorough preparation in understanding the Word of God are often subservient to the more spectacular gifts of the Holy Spirit. Strange and inaccurate interpretations of the truths of the Bible can easily be the result, and the door is open to all kinds of doctrinal excesses. Church splits over peculiar new doctrines (or revived old ones) may then be the next step in the chain of events.

And these results are seen. In Colombia today there are already a number of Pentecostal break-off groups (see chap. 3), and some with very far-out beliefs. A small group broke away from the United Pentecostal Church in the city of Armenia, calling itself "Paloma Blanca" (white dove). Another group of members broke away from the United Pentecostal Church in Palmira and follow the doctrine of one William Brown, who, they believe, is the resurrected John the Baptist—the prophet of God for today who is preparing the bride for Christ's coming. Each convert baptizes himself, since the verb for "be baptized" in Acts 2:38 is in the reflexive in Spanish, and can be taken as "baptize yourself" or "be baptized." While they believe in the Trinity of Persons in the Godhead, the unitarian form of baptism is followed. As an Assemblies of God

pastor said: "It is a complete mixture of doctrines."[1] Their
main belief is that the true bride of Christ is hidden among the
members of the Pentecostal churches, and that they are to
bring them out from these churches to the new movement.

There are other break-off groups, and there will be more,
considering the shallow theological and biblical preparation
and understanding that many of the Pentecostal pastors and
believers have.

> It is a common tendency in non-historical circles to belittle
> and neglect the important task of education. . . . In their stress
> on the evangelization of every creature they have ignored
> that other equally important aspect of the Great Commission,
> to teach. . . . One of the most serious problems facing the
> whole non-historical movement today is its wide-spread de-
> ficiency in the field of education—its lack of well-trained
> national leadership.[2]

The Assemblies of God, however, does emphasize and require formal theological training along with practical experience in the ministry for its pastors, and also places strong
emphasis on the indoctrination of its believers through the
Reglamento. And it is significant that it has not suffered the
break-offs or church splits that some of the other Pentecostal
denominations have experienced. We have also mentioned
that Ignacio Guevara and other leaders in the Panamerican
Mission have recognized, at least to some extent, the problems
that can result from the lack of preparation of their pastors and
leaders, and have at least begun an informal type of Bible
institute to help fill this gap. (See chap. 5.)

Many Pentecostal pastors, however, do not seem to sense
any lack in their theological training, or in the level of biblical
understanding of their people. A question asked of all the
pastors interviewed was, Some are of the opinion that the
Pentecostal churches need a greater theological base. How do
you feel about this? One of three answers was possible: (1) in
complete accord; (2) in partial accord; or (3) not in accord.
Of the Jesus Only pastors interviewed, all chose number (3).

They did not feel any lack in this area. Of the Trinitarian Pentecostal pastors, four felt that there was some truth to the statement, three felt no lack, and two felt that the statement applied to the Jesus Only church but not to them. Among the non-Pentecostal pastors interviewed, all were in full or partial accord that the Pentecostal churches need a greater theological base. But most of them excluded the Assemblies of God from this criticism.

ANTIINTELLECTUAL ATTITUDE

Partly because of the little education that many of the Pentecostal pastors and church members have had, and partly because of the belief that "God has saved us, Jesus is coming and meanwhile the Holy Spirit and the Bible give us all the knowledge we need," there is an antiintellectual attitude on the part of many Pentecostals, especially among the Jesus Only people.

In the questionnaire for members, I asked the informants how much formal education they had received, how much they hoped to give to their children, and what they felt was the minimum education that a pastor should have—no formal education, primary, secondary, or university level. The members interviewed from the United Pentecostal and Panamerican churches averaged between three and four years of primary school. Very few had received any secondary school education. One UPC member said, "Education is not important, but I believe one should learn to read and write." Another expressed a feeling that seems the opposite to what we would expect after conversion: "Since my conversion I have been less concerned about education. But it is important to learn to read." In the non-Pentecostal churches, the average education of the members interviewed was higher, and many had attended secondary school. In the GMU, CMA, Presbyterian, and Baptist churches, most of the young people either were studying, or had studied, in high school, and some were in the university.

A bigger difference showed up, however, in the amount of education that parents hoped to give their children. Most of the United Pentecostal Church members were satisfied to see their children finish primary, most of the Panamerican church members wanted their children to go on to high school, and many of the non-Pentecostal members aspired for their children to go on to college-level studies.

As far as the minimum preparation that a pastor should have, most UPC members felt that primary school was sufficient, and a number felt that no formal education was necessary, as long as the pastor could read and write. About half of the Panamerican members interviewed felt that the pastor should have education at the high school or Bible institute level. These were some of the comments of United Pentecostal and Panamerican church members: "Education doesn't have much to do with the church, because God teaches one. The important things are consecration and the call of God."

"If the pastor is filled with the Spirit and consecrated to Him, he doesn't need much education. Primary school isn't necessary, but knowing how to read and write is."

"I think the pastor can give himself education. The essential thing is to be called of God."
Another expressed what seems like a strange philosophy to most of us, referring to the training a pastor should have: "You don't need so much education for spiritual things, but to get a decent job and make a decent wage, yes." This woman saw the need of education for secular work, but did not think it was necessary for spiritual work in the ministry!

With Pentecostal members, I found a correlation between the amount of education they felt the pastor should have, and the amount that they had received themselves. The more education a member had received, the more he or she felt the pastor should have for the ministry. For example, members that had received some high school education felt that the pastor should also have studies at the high school level. Those who had practically no formal education, felt that the pastor needed less.

In the non-Pentecostal churches, the amount of formal education that the members felt a pastor should have went up considerably. Most members of the GMU, CMA, and some of the Presbyterian churches, felt that a pastor should have at least high school or Bible institute level studies. Most of the Southern Baptist, and some of the Presbyterian members, felt a pastor should have university or seminary level studies.

The lack of preparation of leaders and the antiintellectual attitude in many of the Pentecostal churches have had some adverse results. For one thing, people with a better education will likely not be drawn to a church where the pastor's grammar and messages indicate almost no training. Not only this, but a person with "too much" education may be considered a threat to a pastor and leaders with almost none. Worst of all, this kind of climate stifles the ambition for a better education on the part of the young people coming up in a church.

> Educated members who show intellectual ambitions are watched with considerable suspicion. Since all learning, except knowledge of the Bible, is held to be dangerous to the true faith, very few pastors have been exposed to the teachings of a theological institute.[3]

And if young people do go on and get a good education, they will likely begin turning off to the Pentecostal faith because of its antiintellectual stance. I saw this clearly in one Jesus Only home, where the children have gone on to high school. They are dressing more in the style of young people, and are doubting many of the standards and ideas of their church. Other members will likely interpret this as being a case of too much education and exposure ruining the faith of these young people. But it is more likely that if the standards, teachings, and attitudes of the church were not so extreme, they would not have the desire to leave it. It is this kind of thing that caused a GMU pastor to express that his greatest criticism of the Pentecostal Churches, and especially the Jesus Only church, was,

> their lack of understanding of the value of preparation. I am afraid that many of the children brought up in these churches will not remain in them unless they are kept in the same state of ignorance. Some of these people don't even believe in education, because "everything comes from above."[4]

Again, it is only fair to recognize that there is a difference between Pentecostal denominations. The Jesus Only is most extreme, while the Assemblies of God is emphasizing education more and more. Many of their young people in Bogota are now in high school, and some of them have gone on to the university.

LACK OF INVOLVEMENT IN SOCIAL PROBLEMS

Another related criticism of the Pentecostals is their general lack of involvement in social, community, and national affairs. "They don't have a social consciousness at all, and see no relation between the gospel and the environment in which they live."[5]

One of the criticisms which is being leveled at evangelical churches and missions in general in Latin America is our lack of social concern. Many evangelical leaders admit that we have neglected this aspect of the manifestation of the love of God through His people and His church, and that we have isolated ourselves too much from the very real and pressing social problems in this continent, which is threatened so strongly by revolutionary forces.

> What is the role of evangelical missions in such a continent of ferment? The built-in conservatism of most evangelicals militates against an active participation, or at times even a recognition of, the changing conditions. But missionary strategy even of the 1950's will not suffice for an effective ministry today. The social revolution is pushing missionaries and mission boards into a serious rethinking of their place in Latin American life.
>
> This is not to say that the missionary is no longer called to preach the gospel. The fulfillment of the Great Commission is still his primary task. But in order to reach a people with the gospel he must communicate with them; as Eugene Nida has frequently pointed out, identification is a vital aspect of communication. If Latin Americans do not instinctively feel that we love and understand them in their social as well as their religious aspirations, they will not be willing to listen to what we say.[6]

With this in mind, one of the questions asked pastors was, In your opinion, do you believe that the evangelical church ought to concern itself more with the social problems of the country, and declare itself with respect to these problems? Of fourteen non-Pentecostal pastors interviewed, almost all—twelve of them—answered yes. Trinitarian Pentecostal pastors interviewed were divided about equally in opinion—four answered yes, and three, no. All five of the Jesus Only pastors said no, feeling we should not get involved in the social problems of the country.

I also asked the pastors if they voted in departmental and national elections, and if they encouraged their members to do so. The pattern in the answers was almost the same as for the above question on social concern. Fourteen out of seventeen of the non-Pentecostal pastors interviewed vote and encourage their members to do so. Trinitarian Pentecostal pastors were again equally divided: four out of seven said they do vote, and three out of seven said they encourage their members to do so. Of the Jesus Only pastors interviewed, only one out of five said he votes, and none encourages the members to do so.

Another survey question which was put to the pastors was this: The following is a list of activities that may, or may not, be included in the pastoral ministry. In your opinion, which activities on the list are: (1) very important in the ministry of a pastor; (2) secondary, but included in the ministry of a pastor; (3) excluded from the ministry of a pastor. The list then included the following, and the pastors were to categorize each activity as either 1, 2, or 3.

(*a*) Visit the sick
(*b*) Speak in sermons about the duty of the believer to vote, participate, and know what is happening in local and national government
(*c*) Preach in the church
(*d*) Promote social and community efforts such as schools, clinics, alphabetization, etc.
(*e*) Visit in the hospitals and jails

(*f*) Direct courses of capacitation for lay leaders and Sunday
     school teachers
(*g*) Cooperate with non-Evangelicals in solving social and
     economic problems of common interest (cooperatives,
     Accion Comunal, etc.)
(*h*) Preach in parks, streets, etc.
(*i*) Seek to help members of the church in finding jobs, and
     counselling them on how they can improve their work,
     preparation, and education
(*j*) Speak in sermons about social problems, such as salaries,
     working conditions, illiteracy, etc.
(*k*) Direct special ceremonies such as baptisms, the Lord's
     Supper, etc.

Again, the results followed the same pattern as in the previous questions. The majority of non-Pentecostal pastors felt
that (*b*), (*g*), and (*j*) rated 2, that is, that though they were
secondary, they were a definite part of a pastor's ministry.
Point (*i*) rated as very important in the ministry of a pastor by
almost all of these informants, and (*d*) rated as very important
by half of them, as secondary by the other half.

Trinitarian Pentecostals, on the other hand, were divided as
to whether (*b*), (*g*), and (*h*) formed part of a pastor's ministry
or were completely excluded from it. Point (*d*) was rated as
secondary and point (*i*) as primary, by the majority of these
pastors.

With the Unitarian Pentecostal pastors, any point having to
do primarily with preaching, evangelizing, or directing church
services— (*a*), (*c*), (*e*), (*f*), (*h*), (k)—rated as very important in the ministry, while those having to do with social
problems and involvement were rated as excluded completely
from the ministry—(*b*), (*d*), (*g*), and (*j*). Only one—(*i*)—
which had to do with helping members to find jobs and improve their preparation, rated as secondary, but included in the
ministry.

In the one other question dealing with social and community
affairs, I asked both pastors and members whether they felt an

Evangelical could enter politics, be a member of an athletic team, *Accion Comunal* (community action), a labor union, or a cultural club. Table 12 shows how the informants answered, in terms of the percentages that answered, yes, the Evangelical can participate in such an activity, or no, the Evangelical should not get mixed up in this activity.

TABLE 12

SOCIAL AND COMMUNITY AFFAIRS: PERCENTAGE OF PASTORS AND
MEMBERS THAT APPROVED OF PARTICIPATION IN
THESE ACTIVITIES[a]

ACTIVITY	NON-PENTECOSTALS	TRINITARIAN PENTECOSTALS	JESUS ONLY PENTECOSTALS
Athletic team	83%	34%	0%
Accion Comunal	78%	50%	20%
Politics	64%	6%	0%
Labor union	46%	18%	0%
Cultural club	81%	70%	7%

[a]The sample was made up of: 26 informants from the Jesus Only church, 34—48 from the Trinitarian Pentecostal churches, and 78—125 from the non-Pentecostal Protestant churches.

As the table indicates, 100 percent of the Jesus Only pastors and members interviewed were against any involvement with organized athletics, politics, or labor unions. Only 20 percent approved of participating in community action groups. Trinitarian Pentecostals were equally divided about participating in community action efforts, but most were against being involved in organized athletics, politics, or labor unions. The great majority of the non-Pentecostals, on the other hand, felt that an Evangelical can participate in all of these activities, except labor unions, which in Colombia are known to be quite leftist politically. But even here opinion was quite divided.

> These few evidences indicate that pentecostalism pertains to the Niehburian type, "Christ against culture." . . . The judgment pronounced against society is without appellation: entertainments and athletics, if not the "works of the devil," are at least "time lost in the work of the Lord"; the labor union and political party are "places of perdition."[7]

The weakness in this stand on extreme separation from society and its interests and problems is that Pentecostalism is not in a position to influence society's structure for God. By remaining so apart from community, political, and social activities, it is in one sense supporting the status quo. At the very least, it gives the appearance of being unconcerned about the problems, injustices, and hardships of the people.

> A major criticism of the Pentecostal churches is the fact that they do not participate in the solution to the social and economic problems around us. They are very content in their situation, and as a result, are supporters of the status quo.[8]

With this in mind, Stanley Rycroft wrote:

> We cannot escape the conviction that it is the denominations with a church tradition and consciousness back of them who are going to make a lasting impression on the Latin American people, for they seek to form a Church with roots in the community rather than mere groups of people.[9]

The danger does not seem to lie so much in that they seek to form "mere groups of people," but that so often they form isolated groups of people—separated from the mainstream of society.

But before judging them too harshly at this point, we need to remember that the majority of the Pentecostals have come from the lower and marginal classes of society which have seldom had any voice in the affairs of their country or community, and which have generally suffered at the hands of those who do control the affairs of the society in which they live.

> Do not forget that for Pentecostals, . . . the "world" is, above all and in an experiential way, the world of misery, of sickness, and of death; the origin of its rejection is found in the panic fear of a world in which the new Christian, poor among the poor and marginal among the marginal, has only received deceptions and sufferings. Once again, to whoever doubts these statements, we recommend the work of Oscar Lewis that describes the world of the marginal people.[10]

CAUDILLISMO

Another danger in the Pentecostal movement is that of *caudillismo*. We have already mentioned the concentration of authority in the leaders and pastors of the Panamerican Mission (chap. 5). While this strong authority may be a factor in church growth at the present time, since Ignacio Guevara has proven to be a good leader, and has chosen other good leaders under him, there could be a very real problem later on. "Right now Ignacio is the *caudillo,* and he fills this role well because he is a humble and good leader. But what if others follow him that are not like this?"[11]

The *caudillo* system can be effective with people who are accustomed to this, and when the leaders and pastors fill their role well as worthy men of God. But it also presents opportunities for dictators to arise, for the mismanagement of funds, and for excessive personalism. And in the case of a pastor who is a strong *caudillo* over his congregation, there is the very real possibility of stifling the development of leadership in the church, and of creating resentment as a result.

> The danger I see is this: the day may come when some of the congregations will not accept this kind of dictatorship, and some of the lay leaders in the churches will not be satisfied to take such a back seat. Also, what happens if a pastor arises that is immature, false, headstrong, or proud, and he is given the authority to make all the final decisions?[12]

This seems to have been a part of the problem in the split which took place in the Panamerican Mission in Bogota. When the Panamerican Mission sought to discipline a pastor who was accused of immorality, the pastor, who had such a strong hold over his people, was able to take the whole congregation with him in forming a new church.

> Where small Pentecostal churches grow into large churches, this mentality can be seen being transferred to the "pastor presidente." It can be seen in countless Pentecostal churches where the leaders have great prestige among and control over the church members. Many churches become small

ecclesiastical domains within their denominations, and often personality cults grow up around personality leaders.[13]

Sally Morley, of the United Pentecostal Church, sees the possibility of a dictatorship situation within the Colombian United Pentecostal Church: "A danger that I see is a sort of hierarchy in the general board; there is too much power in this small group."[14]

An example of what I consider an abuse in the *caudillo* system, is the authority that pastors have over money matters in some of the churches. One question that I asked pastors was who managed the money of the church—an official board along with the congregation, or the pastor himself. Most of the United Pentecostal pastors said that they themselves managed the money and largely determined how it was to be spent. Most of them also admitted that no monthly treasurer's report was given in their churches. This means that they operate under the same system as the Roman Catholic church in Colombia: the average member gives without really knowing where his money goes. This opens the door to the strong possibility of abuse of funds on the part of the pastor. In the interviews with the members of the other denominations, almost all of them knew how much their pastor's monthly salary was. But only two out of fifteen Jesus Only members had *an idea* of how much their pastor was taking out of the tithes and offerings for his salary each month. When I asked them how much their pastor's salary was, most of them answered, "I don't know," or, "I'm not sure." I personally cannot conceive of members accepting this kind of pastoral control in a church, but it takes place under the *caudillo* system in the United Pentecostal Church in Colombia. It is this type of thing that prompted Eugene Nida to write:

> No appraisal of the indigenous movements in Latin America can be justly made without a realistic understanding of some of the dangers, for these do exist. For one thing there is the tendency toward *caudillismo*, which might be translated as "irresponsible leadership" or "bossism." These strong

leaders sometimes demand the kind of blind devotion with which the people have been formerly familiar in the Roman Church.[15]

PENTECOSTALISM IS DIVISIVE

Pentecostalism in Colombia has also caused problems where it has entered the non-Pentecostal Protestant churches. We have already mentioned the difficulty that WEC is having in Bogota, and the possible division that this denomination faces over the Pentecostal issue. (See chap. 3.)

The largest Interamerican church in the city of Medellin has suffered a split as a result of Pentecostalism. The pastor had been influenced strongly by the Pentecostal tendencies that have come into the Latin American mission's work in Colombia, and began to campaign for certain Pentecostal manifestations in his church. When the National Association of Interamerican Churches sought to lay down some guidelines regarding the charismatic manifestations, the pastor in question pulled out from the Interamerican church, and took about half of the congregation of the church with him. Later the same pastor threatened to sue the Interamerican Mission for a large sum of money which he felt was owed him for his years of ministry in the Interamerican churches. The whole thing was a nasty affair.[16]

My own mission, the Gospel Missionary Union, has had a few problems as well. For a time it looked as if the church in the city of Tulua might be divided over the matter of tongues, visions, all praying at once, and so on. After a series of special messages on the Holy Spirit, His baptism and gifts, most of the problems ceased. In Palmira, the La Emilia Church also went through a time of difficulties over Pentecostalism. Several believers of Pentecostal persuasion began to attend this GMU church, and won a certain amount of sympathy from several members of the church, as well as the pastor himself. For a while, it looked as though the people who sympathized with Pentecostalism might take the church over completely, including the building. But things came to a head, there were bad feelings, and the believers of Pentecostal persuasion left, taking a number of GMU members with them.[17]

The point in all of these cases is this: when the influence of Pentecostalism has entered a church or denomination which is not Pentecostal, there have been divisions and bad feelings, and the churches have suffered as a result. One Colombian pastor expressed this when he said, "There is a tendency for Pentecostalism to create divisions. In Bogota we have seen something of this, and it isn't a good testimony."[18]

EXCLUSIVISTIC ATTITUDE AND PROSELYTIZING ACTIVITIES

But the thing that probably rankles many Protestant leaders most about the Pentecostal churches is their exclusive attitude toward other Protestant groups and their proselytizing activities.

> The Pentecostal Churches tend to be very judgmental toward other Protestant churches, and consider themselves to be the true church. . . . Making glossalalia and other charismatic manifestations a criterion of spirituality produces an arrogance and pride which is unhealthy.[19]

Dr. George Biddulph adds, speaking of the past struggles and sacrifice in establishing the evangelical church in Colombia:

> The Pentecostals feel they have something no one else has. . . . There is a lack of historical perspective, and Pentecostals generally don't appreciate what the evangelical church has gone through to get where it is now. Some of them have just come in like the wind.[20]

Of course it is the Pentecostal doctrine of the baptism of the Holy Spirit, and the charismatic experiences, that create this "superior" attitude, and the urge to "win" other evangelical believers to their fold. As Boyce Wallace of the Cumberland Presbyterian church expressed it, "It is their proselytizing that bothers us the most. This has its roots in their theology; they feel we need to be won to a higher plane."[21]

Many of the Pentecostal pastors and missionaries have themselves come out of other Protestant churches. Domingo Zuniga of the United Pentecostal Church had first been a Southern Baptist, and Manuel Ospina and his brother Noel, both pastors in the UPC as well, came out of the Gospel Missionary Union. Abelardo Barrera from the Assemblies of God had been with the Christian and Missionary Alliance for a time. Ignacio Guevara and Hector Machuca of the Panamerican Mission, came out from the Interamerican Mission. And among the missionaries, the Harry Bartels had first served with the Mennonite Brethren Mission before affiliating with the Assemblies of God Church. The William Thompsons, of the UPC, had first come to Colombia as missionaries with a Trinitarian holiness group. Sally Morley was converted to Pentecostalism while studying as a Southern Baptist. Since many of the leaders in the Pentecostal denominations were themselves converted to Pentecostalism from other evangelical denominations, they likely will carry the same urge to convert other Evangelicals to their Pentecostal faith.

And the Pentecostals have proselytized. In Palmira, the pastor of the First United Pentecostal church estimates that 30 percent of its members came from other evangelical churches in the city—a total of about 225 proselytes.[22] The second UPC church in Palmira has about forty members that came from other Protestant churches.[23] About one third of the members of the Assemblies of God church here were proselytes from other evangelical churches.[24]

In Pereira, the pastor of the Panamerican church estimated that about twenty members had previously been in other Protestant churches in the city—about 20 percent of their membership.[25] The pastor of the United Pentecostal church in the center of the city said, "There is a good number of people in our church from the Presbyterian, Baptist, Adventist, and Christian and Missionary Alliance churches, as well as former Jehovah's Witnesses."[26] About thirty members of the second United Pentecostal church were proselytes at the time of my interview with the pastor there.[27]

And in Bogota—the third case-study city—the pastor of the Bethel Assemblies of God Church, estimated that about 20

percent of the members came from other evangelical churches
—a total of about fifty.[28]

The Jesus Only people are considered the worst in this, and
they themselves make no bones about it. As far as they are concerned, the other Evangelicals do not have a complete gospel or
experience, and they feel that they are doing other Evangelicals
a great favor by seeking to win them. Domingo Zuniga, a
leader in the United Pentecostal Church who is far more open
than many of them, explained how he feels about other denominations:

> In education there are several levels: primary, secondary,
> college, and post-graduate. All churches that preach re-
> pentance and faith in Christ are Christian. But the difference
> is in the level of spirituality that is attained.[29]

Obviously we are in grade school while they are the post-
graduates, but at least we are at the first level!

If we take these proselytes to Pentecostalism from other
evangelical churches into account, the real church growth
achieved by the Pentecostal churches is reduced somewhat,
since some of this growth simply amounts to a transfer of true
believers from one denomination to another.

MAJOR LESSONS

But having mentioned these negative aspects in the Pentecostal movement and in some of the Pentecostal denominations,
we need to come back to the fact that they *are* the fastest-
growing churches in Colombia; they *are* appealing more to the
common people; they *have* established objectives, strategies,
and methods which are proving effective; and they *are* revived
churches, at least by the definition of revival that we gave in
the last chapter. We can profit from their experience and
growth as we are willing to learn from them, evaluate our own
churches and ministries, and change our thinking and practices where we should do so.

And there is every evidence that many of the Protestant
leaders in Colombia are taking a serious look at what the

Pentecostals are accomplishing and the reasons for it. In the interviews with non-Pentecostal pastors and denominational leaders, I mentioned that in Brazil and Chile and a number of other countries of Latin America, the Pentecostal churches are the strongest, and are growing much faster than the other Protestant churches in these countries. I then asked, "In your opinion, do you think we are heading toward a similar situation in Colombia?" Of twenty-three pastors and leaders, twenty-one answered yes. In other words, they are aware of the rapid growth of the Pentecostal churches in Colombia, and of the trend there. I then asked these same pastors and leaders if they thought we could learn important lessons from the Pentecostals, and if they did, what these lessons were. All of them answered that there were some definite lessons to learn from them, and gave what they considered to be the principal ones. These are listed according to the frequency with which they were mentioned, with the first being the most often mentioned: (1) meetings which are more alive, joyful, and enthusiastic; (2) the mobilization of a greater percentage of the believers in the churches; (3) the opportunity for more people to participate in the services and activities of the church; (4) more emphasis in the churches on the Holy Spirit and His gifts and power; (5) the self-support system in the churches; and (6) a greater emphasis on the apprenticeship system of training pastors and church leaders.

I am convinced that we can significantly increase the growth of our non-Pentecostal churches in Colombia and Latin America without having to become Pentecostal in the process, if we heed what I feel are the principal lessons for us in their growth. What are these lessons?

CHURCH-CENTERED

The first thing which Pentecostal growth teaches us is that our mission methods and efforts must center around the planting, growth, and outreach of local churches. Our success in evangelizing any country depends largely on the extent to which we are able to plant and develop churches which reproduce themselves. In reading the book of Acts, one is impressed that Paul's strategy in each place was not only to evangelize the people who lived there, but also to leave an organized local church. Yet this fact seems to be a hard-learned one for many of us as missionaries, and for many foreign mission boards, as Arthur Glasser emphasizes:

> For years the OMF has been trying to pry itself loose from the concept of evangelism which by-passed the local church. We keep pounding into one another's heads that God's door for the evangelization of the world is the local church. We believe the best door for planting a church is the existing Church.[30]

The problem is that we seem to stray so easily from this scriptural ideal of planting self-propagating churches, into placing emphasis on secondary service institutions and ministries. A missionary leader in Colombia has warned that "the present trend in Colombia is toward specialists not directly involved in the building of congregations." He then recommends that "the Mission should work against this trend, and specialists should be involved in church building and growth."[31] And then there are our many institutions, which while doing a worthy work, may not be contributing very much to planting and building up local churches. Some of them have been allowed to become almost an end unto themselves.

> We know that the biblical goal for missions is soul winning and church planting. Sometimes, when there has not been a ready response to our labors, our efforts have found a substitute channel in institutional work that ministers to the physical and intellectual needs of the people, with little or no church planting as a result.[32]

Once a mission has veered from the primary task of planting and developing churches, to the path of institutionalism, it is not easy for it to get back to the primacy of the church in its thinking and efforts. But it *must* be done, *if* we want to achieve our primary goal. Dr. Wilbert Norton sets forth two important ways in which mission boards can help to assure their sticking to the basic task:

1. Have clear written statements on primary and secondary objectives. The primary task of the mission—church-planting and growth—should be stated so clearly and forcefully that all who are connected with the mission get the message. This includes the board of directors, administration, staff, missionaries, appointees, and if possible, even supporters. There should also be a statement on the role of secondary ministries and institutions, and how they relate and contribute to achieving the mission's basic objectives.

2. Periodic reevaluation. Stated principles are one thing, actual practices on the field are often another. So there is the need of periodic evaluation, on a regular basis, of every ministry and institution in a given country. This evaluation is necessary to see if we *are* actually putting first things first, to see if certain ministries and institutions are really still needed, and whether they are contributing to achieving the mission's stated aims.[33]

One way we can evaluate each ministry and institution is by asking certain questions; the answers will help us to determine whether the ministry or institution in question is worthy of continued support and effort. Some of these questions are:

1. How many converts are there from a particular activity or institution?
2. How does this activity or institution stand up in a cost-personnel ratio, as compared with other efforts of the mission?
3. What kind of converts is this effort or institution producing? Are they mature, durable, reproductive? Is this effort helping to furnish strong Christian leadership to the total church?
4. How does each particular effort or institution relate to the church and its spiritual development, outreach, and multiplication?
5. Is this effort or institution fulfilling the purpose for which it was initiated?[34]

Since the church is God's redeeming agent in the world, it must be central in all our thinking and planning. The Pentecostals in Colombia have realized this. They have not substituted other ministries or institutions for the primary task of planting and developing vital local churches that reproduce themselves. There is no faster or more effective way to evangelize a country.

> The greatest contribution that a missionary can make to world evangelism is to raise up churches that will fulfill their mission to their respective communities. Greater than all other factors for world evangelism, more important than radio, literature, or institutions, as needful as these things are, is the establishment of the Church of Jesus Christ, filled with the Spirit and set on the march to witness. Let us establish, by God's help, multitudes of local churches—living cells of the body of Christ.[35]

MOBILIZED MEMBERS

The second important lesson that the Pentecostal churches in Colombia teach us is that we must find the way to mobilize the members of our churches in continual personal evangelism, and in local church ministries and outreach.

So important is this, that the Latin American Mission team members who authored the book, *Evangelism in Depth*, wrote, "The successful expansion of any movement is in direct proportion to its success in mobilizing and occupying its total membership in constant propagation of its beliefs."[36] At this point we are challenged to examine our attitude:

> Do we think our task is to win all the souls possible in one area and conserve these results by bringing them into a church, and then begin the process again in another area? Do we leave evangelism to a professional class of missionaries and trained pastors, forgetting that the entire Church is composed of children of the Kingdom who are the seed for future harvest?
>
> In those areas in Latin America where the Church has truly progressed it is notable that the entire Church is fruitful

seed. There is always special emphasis on lay activity. Every convert is a witness and every Christian works not only within his church but in outstations and branch Sunday Schools. He is a personal witness of his belief, extending the Church by his work.[37]

Yet we do not seem to be accomplishing this as the Pentecostals are. A number of evangelical leaders and pastors in Colombia frankly admitted in interviews that in many of our churches, the members seem to lack the contagious enthusiasm for witnessing and serving that the Pentecostal members have. How can we overcome this lack? It is here that the methods and experience of the Pentecostal churches can help us.

First of all, our churches must have a self-image conducive to growth. Churches multiply which see that it is their primary task to reproduce and grow. The best time to establish this self-image is when a church is first founded, but even with the oldest churches, we must teach and pray until each local church is gripped by the fact that its primary task is to grow and reproduce by making Christ known to others through its members.

> Too often the spiritual life of our churches has been self-centered, with concern manifested for the personal spiritual and social benefits received from church life instead of a recognition that the Church is the army of the living God, called to make Christ known everywhere.[38]

Second, it is important that we follow the Pentecostals' example in seeking to involve new converts as soon as possible in a basic Bible study and indoctrination course, as well as in some type of witness and service for the Lord, before they have a chance to cool off in their initial ardor. "New converts are more susceptible to a complete revolution of their total way of life than they will be at any later time. Proper instruction in the beginning will set the pattern for church life and multiplication."[39] In the initial indoctrination course, it is important to teach the new believers that witnessing is not an option for the Christian, but that it is every Christian's duty, responsibility, and privilege to share his faith. They must understand that it is normal for them to witness to others of their faith in Christ and of the profound change which He has wrought in their lives. The sooner we teach, train, and motivate new believers for witness and evangelism, the better.

Third, each local church needs to adopt a plan of outreach through which members can be mobilized in an organized way. We have seen that the Assemblies of God has its *campos blancos,* the Foursquare church its branch Sunday schools, the Panamerican Mission its home Bible studies, and the United Pentecostal Church its multiplied preaching points, visitation program, and open-air meetings. In the same way, we need to encourage our churches to adopt a plan of outreach which can be carried on by the members and lay leaders themselves. I personally favor the idea of the *campos blancos* or of somewhat informal home Bible studies. Each church can have several going at a time; some will develop into churches and others will not, but all can help to accomplish two important things: (1) reach the unconverted; and (2) develop Christian lay leaders in the church.

> A church active in evangelistic outreach will become a center which will produce outstations and Christian lay-workers. These outstations may develop into churches and the lay-workers into leaders and pastors. Since these pastors have been raised up in churches which are fervent in soul-winning, they will also have the same vision and will in turn lead their churches in an evangelistic outreach which will result in still more church-planting. Thus the chain-reaction of evangelism and church-planting is put in motion. This is to be our goal.[40]

PROVEN AND PREPARED LEADERS

The third lesson for us in Pentecostal growth is that we must adopt a leadership and pastoral training system which puts as much emphasis on practical experience and proven gifts and leadership, as on academic preparation. The success of the Pentecostal churches in Colombia should certainly cause us to examine our own leadership and pastoral training programs.

These words ring a bell for most of us that have served as missionaries in Latin America:

> Many pastors and workers produced by mission schools
> have neither turned out real soul-winners nor manifested true
> spiritual leadership. . . . Many workers lack initiative and
> depend too much on the mission for guidance and financial
> support. Something has been missing, and it may be that
> neither the missionary nor the worker knows what it is. . . .
> What is this "something" lacking? I often find it can be ex-
> plained by one or more of the following gaps in our training
> program.[41]

Melvin Hodges then suggests four gaps that may exist in our present leadership training methods:

1. A gap may exist between the intellectual and spiritual development of the worker. We may have put too much emphasis on intellectual training and too little on spiritual preparation and maturity.

2. A gap may exist between knowledge and practical ministry. We often place a student in a school in a somewhat artificial environment. He may get out of touch with the real world and its problems. Some students after graduation feel that they are now above pioneering a church or working in a rural area. Certainly there is a measure of failure in a training program which creates an unwillingness to do that which it was our purpose to train them to do.

3. We may have left too wide a gap between the clergy and the laity. Our training program must teach pastors how to enlist the entire church for God.

4. Our concept of the role that training workers plays in the development of the church may be an inadequate one. Some train only to fill pastoral vacancies in existing churches. We must train workers for expansion, which means that we must train more workers than we have churches.[42]

Probably the best solution to the lack of leadership for church outreach and evangelism, and to the economic difficulties of most churches in Colombia, is the training and delegation of responsibility to leading laymen in the different congre-

162   *Explosion of People Evangelism*

gations, so that they can direct outreach efforts in visitation, preaching points, and home Bible studies. Training for these lay leaders should be given in the local-church situation, so that it is on-the-job training. Basic courses in doctrine, church administration, personal evangelism, teaching methods, and homiletics will be helpful.

One way to give this training is through short-term institutes held in centers for the lay leaders within a given region. But even these institutes should not be purely theoretical or academic. In the GMU, we have devised and used a plan for our short-term institutes that we believe has proven effective and fruitful. In a given center where an institute is held, there may be twenty to thirty leaders present from the region. The mornings are dedicated to the study of several subjects, and in the afternoon a class is given on personal evangelism. Then, after prayer, all the students go on a door-to-door visitation ministry, at the same time inviting the townspeople to an open-air meeting for that same night in one of the central plazas. Some of the more capable lay leaders are used in this meeting for special music, testimonies, or a short message. The others are to distribute literature and serve as counsellors. Sometimes evangelistic films are shown. An institute of this kind gives spiritual, academic, and practical training to the participating laymen. It combines theory with practice, as well as making an impact on the community.

Another method of preparing leaders that is already being used by a number of denominations in Colombia is the seminary extension system. It is an autodidactic system using programmed texts, in which lay leaders may receive accredited courses at several levels, according to the amount of schooling they have had. It is on-the-job training, since the students study right where they live and work.

> The "professors" in extension education are really the semi-programmed textbooks which are being written in Spanish to cover the entire theological curriculum. The student applies to the seminary in the usual way, but rather than moving into an institution he remains in his own home and is assigned a

time and place to meet with the human professor who represents the seminary. . . . The teacher checks his work, ex-
amines the student, gives him new assignments, loans him
books, and chats over his problems. This face-to-face, personal contact with the teacher is one of the most obvious differences from a correspondence course.[43]

Most of the students in the seminary extension program will
likely never be full-time paid pastors, but they will serve as lay
leaders in local churches and outstations. Some, however, as
they study and serve, will sense the special call of God on their
lives, and will develop in the ministry to the place where others
will recognize their spiritual gifts and leadership. These will
become pastors of churches. Peter Wagner states part of the
philosophy and advantages of this system:

The new thinking involves another starting point. It does
not start with an established institution, but rather with a man
called of God with spiritual gifts and proven leadership ability
in his church. He may be semi-literate or a university graduate; he may be poor or rich; he may be a farmer or a factory
worker; he may be Indian or criollo—whatever he is, it is
our job to adapt our training program to him, instead of ex-
pecting him to adapt to our training program. In a sense this
might be called humanizing theological education: shifting the
focus from institutions to human beings.[44]

But it is not intended nor expected that the seminary extension program will completely replace the residence theological
schools. It is recognized that these schools also have some
advantages, and that there will be students who have proven
themselves, sense God's call to the ministry, and can afford to
accelerate their training in a residence Bible institute or seminary. The aim, then, in these theological schools is to place as
much emphasis on practical experience in the ministry as on
academic preparation. The Assemblies of God has given us a
good example of this in their Bible institute in Colombia.

We must learn to distinguish between elements of prime
importance and those which are secondary. Proper buildings,

a teaching staff that represents high scholastic achievement, conventional curriculum, methods, length of terms, may be important or may not be important. The point is: do these methods and plans of operation contribute finally to our goal or not? We must be ruthless in eliminating those things that will hinder, as well as progressive and daring in initiating those things that will produce the New Testament Church. . . . We must depend upon the Holy Spirit in the light of the New Testament teaching and on our own experience on the field to indicate to us the way that we should go.[45]

The Christian and Missionary Alliance, in my estimation, approaches this in their Bible institute in Armenia. Students study about seven months out of the year, and the rest of the time many of them are serving as pastors or copastors in different churches. During the school year, classes are set up so that students can leave Friday afternoon for the churches where they are serving, return on Monday, and resume classes on Tuesday. This way students have a long weekend to care for the churches they are pastoring or helping. Most of the GMU students who have attended the CMA Bible institute in Armenia have been able to serve as pastors and leaders in churches at the same time that they were studying. An institute like this trains leaders *in* the ministry and *through* the ministry, not apart from it. And because of the emphasis on practical experience, a student is more likely to be able to tell whether he really has the gifts and calling for the ministry, by the time he is ready to graduate.

Hodges suggests three main objectives for our leadership and pastoral training programs which summarize what we have been saying:

1. We must integrate our training program with the national church. The Bible school or seminary must exist to serve the church and must never be allowed to become or remain an isolated island. The church should feel that the training program of the Bible institute or seminary is its own, that it exists to serve the church, and that its workers are the church's workers.

2. The students must be trained to the task, not away from it! We must avoid sealing off our students from ordinary life and the problems which they will be facing in the ministry later on.

3. We must tailor our training program to fit the need. In Latin America, where many of the converts have modest educational backgrounds, we must have a training program which will enlist them in the cause, as well as a more advanced training program for those who have higher educational qualifications. In other words, we should have schools and seminaries for those who have the qualifications, regional short-term institutes for lay workers, and a training program on the local church level for every member, with the aim being that every member be enlisted in the ministry and evangelistic outreach of the church.[46]

SATISFYING SERVICES

Fourth, we need to ask ourselves how we can adapt our church services so that they more fully meet the spiritual, emotional, and psychological needs of the Colombian people. We have brought out the fact that the Pentecostal church services have more appeal to many of the Colombians than those in the more traditional Protestant churches. This tells us, for one thing, that we need to evaluate our own forms of worship and the format in which we present the gospel, to see whether we have allowed them to be the natural expression of the Colombian church. It is entirely possible that we still hold to a form of church service and a way of presenting the good news, that are more acceptable and relevant to North Americans than to our friends south of the border.

From the Pentecostal experience, we learn that perhaps we need to introduce a little more of the spirit of joy and fiesta in our meetings, instead of what seem like dry lectures to the more emotional Latin Americans.

We must also remember that the Colombian, more than the average North American, loves to act, perform, and participate in public. He seems to feel this impulse and need. Most Colombians would not be very happy for long sitting passively in a pew in the average church service in North America. They want to be seen and heard, and there is nothing wrong with this. But it means that our services must give opportunity for as many as possible to participate, both on the platform and in the pews.

Colombians, as most Latin Americans, also love poetry and drama, so we should encourage their use in church services. Colombians love skits, especially if costumes are involved. Not only do they love to give them, but they also enjoy seeing them. Few services attract so much attention as a good drama. And this has important significance for our preaching as well. If we want to have effective sermons, we should put emphasis on Bible personalities and their struggles, example, and victories.

> The Latin soul is hungry for real spiritual nourishment, not for predigested sermon outlines. They crave realistic portrayals of the great heroes of faith: Abraham, who dared to go into an unknown land in answer to God; Moses, who faced the challenge and the danger of identification with a despised minority; Joshua, who declared himself and his family for God in the midst of mounting opposition from jealous, rebellious followers; David, who conquered a nation but fell victim to his own lust; Jeremiah, who spoke for God the truth that hurt, not only others but himself—and so it goes. The Bible is a book of life, for it comes out of the context of life and is addressed to life. It must not be disguised by our Protestant doctrinal formulations any more than the face of God should be hidden by elaborate ritual of the Roman Church.[47]

After reading some of Nida's articles and books, I personally sought to put this into practice in many of the messages I gave in Colombia. And I believe I can say that many of the messages which God has used the most and which have most effectively reached the hearts of the people, have centered around exciting and dynamic persons and stories of the Bible.

Then there is the whole matter of music, and here some missionaries (and sometimes nationals who have been properly taught and indoctrinated!) become very uptight about the idea of popular or folkloric rhythms being used in the churches. Yet, is it not possible that the Holy Spirit can speak to the Colombian people more effectively through their own music forms, than through music imported from North America or Europe? As missionaries, we should encourage musically gifted Colombian believers to write hymns and choruses in acceptable indigenous forms, and we should encourage the use of hymns and hymnals that incorporate Latin American and national rhythms and lyrics. Eugene Nida draws our attention to the fact that the hymns we sing in the churches in Latin America are often "foreign importations, in which the words are didactic (they teach a lesson) rather than lyric (expressing a sentiment of the heart, as in Spanish and Portuguese poetry and song)."[48]

All of what we have been saying up to this point leads us to a very important conclusion: it is vital that all missionaries and missionary appointees read and study all they can in the areas of church growth, the philosophy of missions and the indigenous church, and the culture they expect to be working in. The more that we understand the culture in which we are ministering, or hope to minister in the future, the more likely it will be that we shall be able to communicate effectively to the people within that culture. It seems rather strange that foreign mission boards usually require a good educational background of all candidates but sometimes neglect to insist that every appointee have at least a basic knowledge in the areas of missions that we have just mentioned. After all, for a missionary, missions *is* his business, and often is his or her lifework. As missionaries, we need to pursue as full an understanding of missions and all this involves as we would in medicine if we were doctors, or in science and physics if we were engineers.

RENEWAL AND REVIVAL

In closing, there is one more major lesson that Pentecostal church growth teaches us, something which goes beyond objectives, methods, or sociological factors. That lesson is, that if our churches are to grow, reproduce, and effectively reach their fellow Colombians for Christ, they must be revived churches.

The greatest need in some of our churches in Colombia is spiritual renewal and revival. Unless we learn in our churches to pray in earnest and trust the Holy Spirit in all areas of the church's life and ministry, all of our methods, strategies, and activities will accomplish very little. Our theme and our goal must be: every church a revived church and every believer a disciple—faithful in Bible study, in prayer, in witnessing, in giving, in serving. The Pentecostals have no special secret of prayer and no exclusive hold on the blessing and power of the Holy Spirit, but they seem to be availing themselves more fully of these divine privileges and provisions. They are an example to us to seek the Lord more fully and serve Him more faithfully, until we experience greater church growth in our own denominations and churches.

> To those brought up in the cloistered shelter of a respectable time-hallowed tradition it may pose a baffling question as to why groups which they consider deficient, shallow and extremist should nevertheless prosper and grow. The answer seems to be that God is no respecter of persons. He is not willing that any should perish. He will have the good news of redemption proclaimed to every creature. He will do it through faulty and defective instruments if He can find no others. He prefers imperfect and immature but living witnesses to impeccably orthodox and correct but slumbering church members.[49]

Appendix

A. HISTORY

1. When was the church founded?
2. How was it founded?
3. Why did you choose this city and *barrio* for a new church?
4. What were the principal methods you used to win new people in the beginning?
5. When did you build the church building? Did you receive financial help from churches in North America, or from the foreign mission? With how much did they help?

B. STATISTICS

1. What has been the membership and average attendance of the church since its founding to the present, especially since 1960?
2. What is the present average attendance for the following: Sunday school, Sunday night, prayer meeting, young people's meeting.
3. How many Sunday school classes are there?
4. What is your average monthly tithes and offerings?

C. MEMBERSHIP

1. What are the requirements for membership?
2. What are the requirements for a member to be considered active?
3. How many on the membership list are active and in fellowship with the church at present?
4. What kind of records of membership does the church keep?
5. How many of the members were previously members of other evangelical denominations? Why did they make this change?
6. What percentage of the members know how to read?

7. How many of the members have studied in high school? University?
8. What are the occupations of most of your members?

D. EXTENSION

1. What have been the most fruitful methods that your church has used to reach new people?
2. How many evangelistic campaigns have you had in the last year? How do you get new people to attend the campaigns?
3. Do you have healing campaigns? How many are usually healed in these campaigns? What place does healing have in attracting and winning new people to the church? Do the majority of cases of divine healing take place in church meetings and campaigns, or in homes?
4. Does your church have branch Sunday schools? How many? Where do you have them? Who directs these?
5. Does your church have preaching points or *campos blancos?* How many? Where do you have them? Who directs them?
6. Does your church have a visitation plan? From door to door? How often do you go out in this plan? How many participate, on an average? How much success have you had in these visitation efforts? Is it one of the church's best methods for growth?
7. Does your church hold open-air meetings? Where? How often? Who directs in these efforts? How much success have you had through these meetings?
8. On an average, how many make decisions for Christ in your church, each week? Each month?
9. How many baptisms have you had in your church in the past month? Year?

E. FOLLOW-UP, INDOCTRINATION, AND PARTICIPATION OF NEW
   BELIEVERS

1. Does your church have a definite plan of follow-up? What is this plan?
2. Does your church have a definite plan for teaching and indoctrinating new believers? Give a brief description of this plan.
3. What are the requirements and the preparation for baptism? Do you have special baptismal classes? How soon after a

person is converted do you seek to initiate him in these classes? How long does it take to finish these baptismal studies?

4. How soon after a person's conversion can he be baptized?
5. Do you teach illiterate members to read in your church?
6. In what activities can new believers participate in your church?

F. THE PASTOR: HIS PREPARATION AND MINISTRY

1. What is your age? Civil status? How many children?
2. For how long have you been a pastor?
3. Have you always belonged to the denomination you are with now? If not, with which denomination were you affiliated previously? Why did you leave that denomination?
4. The following is a list of activities that may or may not be included in the pastoral ministry. In your opinion, which activities on the list are (1) very important in the ministry of a pastor; (2) secondary but included in the ministry of a pastor; (3) excluded from the ministry of a pastor:
   a) Visit the sick
   b) Speak in sermons about the duty of the believer to vote, participate, and know what is happening in local and national government
   c) Preach in the church
   d) Promote social and community efforts such as schools, clinics, alphabetization, etc.
   e) Visit in the hospitals and jails
   f) Direct leadership training courses for lay leaders and Sunday school teachers, etc.
   g) Cooperate with non-Evangelicals in solving social and economic problems of common interest (i.e., cooperatives, *Accion Comunal,* etc.)
   h) Preach in parks, street meetings, etc.
   i) Help members of the church find jobs, and counsel them on how they can improve their work, preparation, and education
   j) Speak in sermons about social problems, such as salaries, working conditions, illiteracy, etc.
   k) Direct special ceremonies such as baptisms, the Lord's Supper, etc.
5. Do you prepare your sermons beforehand almost always, sometimes, or seldom?

6. Do you use helps, besides the Bible, in preparing your sermons? Which ones?

7. On which five of these themes do you preach most often?

Blood of Christ	Tithes and offerings
Sin and repentance	Divine healing
Holiness in the life of the believer	Our duty to witness to others
Holy Spirit	Creation
Second coming of Christ	The church
Mission of the church	The consecration of the believer

8. What does the word *theology* mean to you?
   a) Human ideas of pastors that are too educated and don't understand the real needs of the people and the church.
   b) Trusting in the thinking and writings of men instead of letting the Holy Spirit teach one directly from the Bible.
   c) The systematic and thorough study of the Word of God.

9. Some are of the opinion that the churches of Pentecostal doctrine lack in theology. What is your opinion on this?

10. Do you believe that it is all right for an Evangelical to be a member of an athletic team? *Accion Comunal?* Political party? Labor union? Social or cultural club?

11. In your opinion, do you think that the evangelical church ought to concern itself more with the social problems of the country, and declare itself with respect to these problems?

12. Do you vote in the elections? Do you encourage the members of your church to vote?

13. How did you become a pastor? What training and apprenticeship did you have before becoming a pastor?

14. What education and preparation have you had? How many years of primary? Secondary? University? Bible institute or seminary?

15. What other preparation and study would you like to have for the pastorate? What insufficiencies do you feel in the ministry, with respect to education and preparation?

G. LEADERSHIP IN THE CHURCH

1. Does your church have an official board or deacons?
2. How are the members of this board elected?

3. Who directs the church?
4. Does your church have an official treasurer that is not the pastor? Does he give monthly reports to the church?
5. Is the money that enters in tithes and offerings money that the church or board of officials handles or money that the pastor handles?
6. Does your church have lay preachers? How many? Where do they preach?
7. How can one become a lay preacher in your church?
8. What kind of further preparation and training do you give those who are already lay preachers?

H. MEETINGS

1. How many meetings does your church have a week, and when?
2. Which meetings are best attended? Which generate the most enthusiasm?
3. Who directs the different meetings?
4. In what ways can the congregation participate in the meetings?
5. What music do you have in your church? (choir, groups, instruments, etc.).
6. How often do you have visiting special speakers in the church? Who are they as a rule?
7. If this is the central church in this city, what is the relation between this church and the rest of the churches in the city and in neighboring towns?

I. DISCIPLINE AND STANDARDS

1. What code or written standards do you have for members?
2. How do you proceed if a member is accused of violating one of these standards?
3. What disciplinary measures are taken if a member is found guilty?
4. In your opinion, what are the most serious sins that a Christian can commit?
5. What sins have caused most problems in your church?

J. MISSIONARIES AND THE FOREIGN MISSION

1. What part do missionaries have in *your* church?

2. In your opinion, what ought to be the main ministries of missionaries in Colombia today?
3. Does this church receive financial subsidy from churches in North America? The foreign mission? A general fund of the national churches in Colombia? How much help do you receive and for what purposes? (salary of the pastor, rent, general expenses, etc.).
4. What ties and fellowship do you feel in your church, with your own denomination in other parts of the world?

K. PROBLEMS IN THE CHURCH

1. In your church, are there groups that oppose each other? Over what matters?
2. What are the principal problems that have impeded greater growth in your church, and how can these problems be overcome?

L. SUPPLEMENT ON THE PENTECOSTAL CHURCHES (for non-Pentecostal pastors only)

1. In your opinion, why are the Pentecostal churches growing so fast?
2. Which factors could we incorporate with profit in our churches, and to what extent could we do so?
3. How many members from your church have you lost to the Pentecostal churches? Why did they leave? What kind of believers were they before they left (zealous, faithful, active, problematical, unstable, etc.)? After they left, did they seek to take other members of your church with them?
4. What are your main criticisms of the Pentecostal movement and churches? What do you see as their main weaknesses?
5. You are aware that the main preparation of the pastors in some of the Pentecostal denominations is practical experience, and that as a man gains more experience and has success in his ministry, he is promoted to a higher level in the ministry. Do you think that this system presents some advantages over the system of preparing pastors in Bible institutes or seminaries? If your answer is yes, do you feel that we ought to incorporate some aspects of this system in our method of preparing pastors? Which aspects?

6. In Brazil and Chile and in some of the other countries of Latin America, the Pentecostal churches are the strongest, and are growing more rapidly than the other Protestant churches in these countries. In your opinion, do you think that we are heading for a similar situation in Colombia? Why do you feel this way?

7. Do you believe that we can learn some important lessons from the Pentecostal churches and their growth? Which lessons, primarily?

QUESTIONNAIRE FOR DENOMINATIONAL DIRECTORS

A. STATISTICS

1. How many organized churches do you have in Colombia? Preaching points or *campos blancos?* Ordained pastors? Non-ordained pastors?

2. What is the total membership of your denomination in Colombia?

3. What is the total attendance of all your churches in the principal meeting of the week?

B. INSTITUTIONS

1. Does your church or mission in Colombia sponsor any of the following?
   a) Primary schools—How many?
   b) High schools—How many?
   c) Bible institute—Where?
   d) Seminary—Where?
   e) Hospital—Where?
   f) Bookstores—How many?
   g) Printing press—Where?
   h) Radio programs—How many?
   i) Orphanage—Where?

2. Does your denomination have its own magazine or publication in Colombia? What other special literature does your denomination produce and use?

3. If your church in Colombia has a Bible institute or seminary, what are the entrance requirements in regard to age and education? Spiritual life? Practical experience in the ministry?

4. How many students do you have enrolled this year?
5. How many years of study before one can graduate? What is the length of school term each year?
6. What do the students do between school terms?
7. What do the majority of the students do after graduation?
8. What steps or levels are there in the ministry in your denomination, and how does a person move up from one level to another?

C. CONFERENCES

1. In your denomination, do you have conferences during the year to which you invite all the members of your churches? For pastors and leaders?
2. How often do you have them?
3. How many attended the last conference?
4. What are the main purposes of these conferences?

D. MISSIONARIES, NATIONAL AND FOREIGN

1. Has your church in Colombia sent national missionaries to other regions of the country? How many? Where?
2. Has your church in Colombia sent national missionaries to other countries? How many? Where?
3. How many foreign missionaries are serving in your denomination or mission in Colombia? Where, and in what capacity are they serving?
4. In your opinion, what ought to be the principal ministries of your missionaries in Colombia today?
5. In your opinion, what have been the principal factors in the growth (or nongrowth) of your churches in Colombia? (methodological, sociological, and doctrinal factors).
6. What have been the main problems that have impeded greater growth in your churches in Colombia?
7. Foreign missionaries: what preparation did you receive before coming to Colombia, in the science and philosophy of mission, in strategy, and in church-growth studies? What uniform preparation and orientation in mission do you require of new missionaries, before and after they arrive in Colombia?

E. SUPPLEMENT ON THE PENTECOSTAL CHURCHES (for non-Pentecostal directors only):

1. In your opinion, why are the Pentecostal churches growing so fast? (factors in their growth).
2. Which of these factors could we incorporate with profit in our churches, and to what extent could we do so?
3. What are your main criticisms of the Pentecostal movement and churches? What do you see as their main weaknesses?
4. Generally the pastors of your denomination are prepared in a Bible institute or seminary where they study for several years and later take a pastorate. Do you think that this system of preparing pastors fills the needs of the churches and the evangelical work in Colombia? If not, why not?
5. You are aware that the main preparation of the pastors in some of the Pentecostal denominations is practical experience, and that as a man gains more experience and has success in the ministry, he is promoted to a higher level in the ministry. Do you think that this system of preparing pastors presents some advantages over that of preparing them in Bible institutes or seminaries? If your answer is yes, do you feel that we ought to incorporate some aspects of this system in our method of preparing pastors? Which aspects?
6. In Brazil and Chile and in some of the other countries of Latin America, the Pentecostal churches are the strongest, and are growing more rapidly than the other Protestant churches in these countries. In your opinion, do you think that we are heading for the same situation in Colombia?
7. Do you believe that we can learn some important lessons from the Pentecostal churches and their growth? Which lessons, primarily?

QUESTIONNAIRE FOR CHURCH MEMBERS

A. HISTORY

1. For how long have you lived in this city?
2. Where did you live previously?
3. Why did you move to this city? Did your moving have to do with *La Violencia?*
4. Did you like the city and life here when you arrived?

5. Were you a Pentecostal when you came to this city?
6. In what *barrio* do you live?
7. Do you have a job at the present time? What is your job?
8. Are you married? Do you live with your spouse? How many children do you have?

B. EXPERIENCE

1. When did you become a believer?
2. What denomination or church did you belong to before?
3. Who won you to your faith? (pastor, evangelist, another believer, radio, literature).
4. Do you have assurance that you are saved? How do you know?
5. Which of your beliefs are most important *to you?*
6. Which three do you like *most* about your own church?
   a) The doctrine
   b) The wonderful and personal experiences through the Holy Spirit
   c) The opportunity to serve and participate
   d) The feeling of warmth and fellowship in the church
   e) The pastor and his preaching
   f) The standards that the church has
   g) Other
7. Which is your favorite meeting of the week? Why?
8. As a rule, how many meetings do you attend each week?
9. Do you believe that your church is more spiritual than the other evangelical churches in this city? Why?
10. Have you experienced the baptism of the Spirit? What was this experience like?
11. Have you experienced divine healing? How and from what have you been healed?
12. Have you spoken in tongues? What was this experience like, and what did it mean to you?
13. Have you had visions or dreams from the Lord? What were they?

C. SERVICE AND ACTIVITIES

1. What responsibilities do you have in the church? In preaching points, branch Sunday schools?

2. Do you tithe? Why?
3. Do you speak to others about your faith? Does your church encourage you to witness? How?
4. How many of your relatives, friends, and neighbors have you won to your faith?
5. In your opinion, what is the best of the following ways for your church to win others and grow: campaigns, meetings in homes, visitation, or personal witness?

D. THE PASTOR

1. Does your church have a full-time pastor?
2. What do you like best about your pastor, and how has he helped you the most in your life?
3. In your opinion, what is the ministry of a pastor?
4. What do you pay your pastor monthly as a church?
5. Is there something about your church that you don't like, or that you would like to see changed?

E. EDUCATION

1. How do you feel about education?
2. How much education do you have?
3. Do you have children that are studying in primary? high school? university?
4. What plans do you have for the future education of your children?
5. What do you feel is the minimum education that a pastor should have?

F. STANDARDS

1. Do you believe that it is all right for an Evangelical to be a member of an athletic team? *Accion Comunal?* Political party? Labor union? Cultural or social club?
2. In your opinion, do you feel it is all right for a believer to attend the theater? Drink wine occasionally? Dance? Cut her hair (ladies)? Use makeup (ladies)? Dress in style (ladies)? Attend a soccer game?

Notes

CHAPTER 1

1. *1972 World Almanac* (New York: Newspaper Enterprise, 1971), s.v. "Colombia."
2. William R. Read, Victor M. Monterroso, Harmon A. Johnson, *Latin American Church Growth*, p. 124.
3. *Encyclopedia Americana* (1951), s. v. "Colombia."
4. *1972 World Almanac*, s. v. "Colombia."
5. "Facts of a Field: Colombia," *World Vision Magazine*, April 1971, p. 22.
6. Ibid.
7. Gustavo Perez and Isaac Wust, *La Iglesia en Colombia*, p. 171.
8. *Report on Baptist Church Growth in Colombia*, p. 3.
9. "Facts of a Field," p. 22.
10. James Fonseca, *Latin America: A Challenge to Catholics* (Washington: National Catholic Welfare Conference, 1960), p. 14.
11. *Report on Baptist Church Growth*, p. 4.
12. Francisco Ordonez, *Historia del Cristianismo Evangelico en Colombia*, p. 16.
13. Ibid., pp. 361-62.
14. James E. Goff, *Censo de la Obra Evangelica en Colombia: 1966*, 1:1.
15. Ibid.
16. *Report on Baptist Church Growth*, p. 7.
17. Goff, *Census of Protestant Church Members in Colombia: 1969* (Bogota: CEDEC, 1969), p. 1.
18. Ibid.

CHAPTER 2

1. W. R. Read, V. M. Monterroso, H. A. Johnson, *Latin American Church Growth*, p. 58.
2. J. E. Goff, *Censo de la Obra Evangelica: 1966*, pp. 3-4.
3. J. E. Goff, *Census of Protestant Church Members: 1969*, Appendix 1.

CHAPTER 3

1. F. Ordonez, *Historia del Cristianismo Evangelico en Colombia*, pp. 41-51.
2. Dr. Robert Lazear, in an interview, Bogota, July 13, 1971.
3. Ordonez, pp. 43, 44, 128.
4. Ibid., p. 238.
5. Ralph Hines, in an interview, Bogota, July 12, 1971.
6. Ibid.
7. Ibid.
8. Ibid.
9. *Report on Baptist Church Growth in Colombia*, p. 17.
10. Ordonez, pp. 233-34.
11. Glen Kramer, past supervisor of the Assemblies of God in Colombia, in an interview, Bogota, March 12, 1969.
12. Pedro Gutierrez, pastor of the central church of the Interamerican Mission in Bogota, in an interview, Bogota, July 12, 1971.

Notes   181

13. Ed Murphy, of Overseas Crusades in Colombia, in an interview, Cali, April 9, 1970.
14. Domingo Zuniga, past director of the UPC, in an interview, Pereira, April 12, 1969.
15. Ricardo Moreno, in an interview, Bogota, July, 1971.
16. John Thomas Nichol, *Pentecostalism*, pp. 137-39.
17. Luis Eduardo Moreno, founder of the Church of God of Prophecy, in an interview, Bogota, July, 1971.
18. Ordonez, pp. 221-22.
19. Gabriel Velez, in an interview, Pereira, May, 1968.
20. Ray Zuercher and Jose Rengifo, GMU field chairman and vice-president of the GMU Colombian church, respectively, in interviews, Cali, April, 1968.
21. Ordonez, pp. 187-88, 201-210.
22. David Overmoyer, CMA missionary, in an interview, Pereira, January, 1969.
23. Abelardo Barrera, an Assemblies of God pastor, in an interview, Pereira, January 20, 1969.
24. Charles P. Chapman, *With the Bible Among the Andes,* pp. 93-98.
25. Ordonez, pp. 148-50.
26. Lewis and Sally Morley, missionaries with the UPC foreign mission board, in an interview, Cali, May, 1971.
27. Nichol, p. 118.
28. Sally Morley.
29. Ibid.
30. Ibid.
31. Jesus Cardozo, pastor of the central UPC church in Palmira, in an interview, Palmira, November 9, 1970.
32. Jose Tascon, pastor of the second UPC church in Palmira, in an interview, Palmira, November 12, 1970.
33. Josue Salazar, a GMU pastor, in an interview, Palmira, March 17, 1971.
34. Romulo Jimenez, an Assemblies of God pastor, in an interview, Palmira, Mar. 11, 1971.

CHAPTER 4

1. J. T. Nichol, *Pentecostalism,* pp. 1-2.
2. Ibid., p. 7.
3. Ignacio Vergara, *El Protestantismo en Chile,* p. 125.
4. Prudencio Damboriena, *El Protestantismo en America Latina,* 2:245.
5. *Constitucion,* p. 5.
6. Alfonzo Villa, UPC member, in an interview, Pereira, November 25, 1969.
7. *Manual de Doctrina y Practica Cristianas,* p. 18.
8. Segismundo Moreno, in an interview, Pereira, October 8, 1969.
9. Guillermo Valencia, in an interview, Palmira, November 17, 1970.
10. Jesus Londono, UPC member, in an interview, Pereira, November 25, 1969.
11. *Constitucion,* p. 6.
12. Oscar Vouga, "Nuestro Mensaje Evangelico," pp. 20-21.
13. Hernando Betancourt, in an interview, Pereira, November 12, 1969.
14. Alfonzo Villa, in an interview, November 25, 1969.
15. Carmen de Escobar, UPC member, in an interview, Palmira, November 25, 1970.
16. Jesus Londono.
17. *Manual de Doctrina y Practica,* p. 19.
18. Harold Horton, *The Gifts of the Spirit* quoted in Nichol, p. 76.
19. Robert Stevens, *Los Primeros Rudimentos,* lesson 57.
20. Emilio Jimenez, in an interview, Palmira, December 14, 1970.
21. Maria de Betancourt, in an interview, Pereira, November 12, 1969.
22. Hernando Betancourt.
23. Donald McGavran, *Church Growth in Mexico,* pp. 114-15.
24. Jesus Cardozo, in a sermon, May 2, 1971.
25. Damboriena, 2:246.

26. Vergara, p. 125.
27. John J. Considine, *New Horizons in Latin America,* p. 253. For an interesting study on Pentecostal services in America, see William W. Wood, *Culture and Personality Aspects of the Pentecostal Holiness Religion.*
28. Nichol, p. 226.
29. John Mackay, *The Other Spanish Christ,* pp. 247-48.
30. *Manual: Iglesia Pentecostal Unida de Colombia* (Editorial Sigma: Pereira, Colombia, 1967), p. 10.
31. Nichol, p. 90.
32. Vouga, p. 17.
33. Nichol, pp. 90-91.
34. *Manual: Iglesia Pentecostal Unida de Colombia,* p. 8.

CHAPTER 5

1. Glen Kramer, in an interview, Bogota, February 13, 1969.
2. Ibid.
3. Ibid.
4. Ibid.
5. Pedro Ramirez, pastor of the Bello Horizonte Church, in an interview, Bogota, July 10, 1971.
6. Gonzalo Castano, in an interview, Cali, March 3, 1970.
7. Glen Kramer. For more information on the experiences referred to in El Salvador, see Melvin Hodges, "Spiritual Dynamics in El Salvador," *Evangelical Missions Quarterly,* 2 (Winter, 1966):80-83.
8. Glen Kramer.
9. Ibid.
10. *Constitucion,* p. 17.
11. Everett Divine, in an interview, Cali, April 24, 1971.
12. Ibid.
13. Ibid.
14. Ed Murphy, in an interview, Cali, April 9, 1970.
15. Ruperto Velez, in an interview, Cali, November 6, 1970.
16. Donald Fults, Overseas Crusades in Colombia, in an interview, Cali, April 29, 1971.
17. Hector Machuca, in an interview, Bogota, July 10, 1971.
18. Ignacio Guevara, founder of the Panamerican Mission, in an interview, Pereira, February 24, 1970.
19. Hector Machuca.
20. Ignacio Guevara.
21. Ed Murphy.
22. Donald Fults.
23. Ignacio Guevara.
24. Ibid.
25. Ed Murphy.
26. W. R. Read, V. M. Monterroso, H. A. Johnson, *Latin American Church Growth,* p. 321.
27. Ignacio Guevara.
28. Ed Murphy.
29. Ignacio Guevara.
30. Ibid.
31. Ibid.
32. Ed Murphy.
33. Ignacio Guevara.
34. Raymond Becker, quoted in J. T. Nichol, *Pentecostalism,* p. 121.
35. Ed Murphy.
36. Ruperto Velez.
37. Ed Murphy.
38. Humberto Blandon, in an interview, Medellin, April 4, 1970.

39. Uriel Trejos, lay leader of a Foursquare church in an interview, Pereira, February 27, 1970.
40. Ruperto Velez.
41. Uriel Trejos.
42. Humberto Blandon.
43. Domingo Zuniga, in an interview, August 12, 1969.
44. Sally Morley, in an interview, May, 1971.
45. Cornelia Flora, "History of the United Pentecostal Church in Colombia," p. 39.
46. Lewis and Sally Morley, in an interview, May, 1971.
47. Flora, pp. 4-5.
48. Ibid., pp. 7-8.
49. Sally Morley.
50. Lewis Morley.
51. Ibid.
52. Domingo Zuniga.
53. Ibid.
54. Ibid.
55. Flora, p. 36.
56. Gabriel Velez, in an interview, Pereira, May, 1968.
57. Domingo Zuniga.
58. Abelardo Galvis, pastor of the second UPC church in Pereira, in an interview, Pereira, September 4, 1969.
59. Ibid.
60. Domingo Zuniga.
61. Manuel Ospina, in an interview, Pereira, January, 1969.
62. Jesus Cardozo, in an interview, Palmira, November 9, 1970.
63. Flora, p. 7.
64. Sally Morley.
65. Ibid.
66. Ibid.
67. Manuel Bernal, in an interview, Pereira, November 25, 1969.
68. Manual Ospina.
69. Domingo Zuniga.
70. Gordon Lindsay, quoted in Nichol, p. 222.
71. Nichol, p. 222.
72. Carlos Moreno, UPC pastor, in an interview, Pereira, September 8, 1969.
73. Manuel Ospina.
74. Octavio Moreno, in an interview, Bogota, July 14, 1971.
75. Pablo Mendoza, in an interview, Pereira, September 3, 1969.
76. From a flyer announcing an evangelistic campaign in Armenia.
77. Abelardo Barrera, in a sermon, October 30, 1968.
78. Ibid.
79. Eugene Nida, "The Indigenous Churches in Latin America," *Practical Anthropology,* 8 (May-June, 1961):102.
80. Dr. George Biddulph, director of the Interamerican Mission, in an interview, Medellin, December 1, 1970.
81. Ray Zuercher, GMU field chairman, in an interview, April 11, 1970.
82. Dr. Alan Neely, professor at the Southern Baptist Seminary in Cali, in an interview, November 23, 1970.
83. Rev. Ralph Hines, in an interview, July 12, 1971.
84. Belarmino Dusan, a Southern Baptist pastor, in an interview, Pereira, March 7, 1970.
85. Maria Betancourt, in an interview, Pereira, November 12, 1969.
86. Abelardo Galvis, UPC pastor, in an interview, Pereira, September 4, 1969.
87. Octavio Moreno.
88. Ruperto Velez, in an interview, November 6, 1970.
89. Jesus Cardozo, in a sermon, May 2, 1971.
90. Ed Murphy.

91. Ibid.
92. Manuel Ospina.
93. Charles S. Snyder, Jr., "Pentecostals," *Missionary Messenger,* September, 1969, p. 21.
94. Eugene Nida, "Communication of the Gospel in Latin America with Special Reference to Christian Literature and Radio" (a mimeographed study), pp. 7-8.
95. Ed Murphy.
96. Glen Kramer.
97. *Constitucion,* p. 1.
98. *Report on Baptist Church Growth in Colombia,* p. 26.
99. Lewis Morley.
100. Glen Kramer.
101. Aldemar Pardo, of the Bible Societies, in an interview, Cali, May, 1971.
102. Ignacio Guevara.
103. Aldemar Pardo.
104. Belarmino Dusan.
105. Donald Fults.
106. Read, Monterroso, Johnson, p. 321.
107. Dr. Alan Neely.
108. Read, Monterroso, Johnson, p. 321.
109. Ed Murphy.
110. Franz Aguirre, a GMU pastor, in an interview, Palmira, January 20, 1971.
111. Eugene Kelly, in an interview, Cali, November 19, 1970.
112. Jesus Cardozo.
113. Octavio Moreno.
114. Ed Murphy.
115. George Biddulph.
116. Pedro Ramirez.
117. Clara de Villa, in an interview, Pereira, January 13, 1970.
118. Omar Aguirre, in an interview, Pereira, October 7, 1969.
119. Franz Aguirre.

CHAPTER 6

1. Romulo Jimenez, in an interview, March 11, 1971.
2. Kenneth Strachan, *The Missionary Movement of the Non-Historical Groups in Latin America,* p. 10.
3. William D'Antonio and Fredrick Pike, *Religion, Revolution, and Reform* (N. Y.: Frederick Praeger, 1964), p. 106.
4. Josue Salazar, in an interview, Cali, November 20, 1970.
5. Dr. Alan Neely, in an interview, Cali, November 23, 1970.
6. C. Peter Wagner, "Today's Missions in the Latin American Social Revolution," *Evangelical Missions Quarterly,* 1 (Winter, 1965):19-20.
7. Lalive d'Epinay, *El Refugio de las Masas* (Santiago, Chile: Editorial del Pacifico, 1968), p. 157.
8. Josue Salazar.
9. Stanley Rycroft, *Religion and Faith in Latin America* (Philadelphia: Westminster, 1958), p. 92.
10. Lalive d'Epinay, p. 158.
11. Ruperto Velez, in an interview, July 9, 1971.
12. Ibid.
13. William R. Read, *New Patterns of Church Growth in Brazil* (Grand Rapids: Eerdmans, 1965), p. 212.
14. Sally Morley, in an interview, May, 1971.
15. Eugene Nida, "The Indigenous Churches in Latin America," p. 104.
16. Dr. George Biddulph, in an interview, December 1, 1970.
17. Gentil Soto, interview, Palmira, Nov. 25, 1970.

18. Armando Hernandez, a non-Pentecostal pastor, in a questionnaire reply, April 3, 1970.
19. Dr. Alan Neely.
20. George Biddulph.
21. Boyce Wallace, in an interview, Cali, November 4, 1970.
22. Jesus Cardozo, in an interview, November 9, 1970.
23. Jose Tascon, in an interview, November 12, 1970.
24. Romulo Jimenez, in an interview, March 11, 1971.
25. Carlos Moreno, in an interview, September 8, 1969.
26. Manuel Ospina, in an interview, January, 1969.
27. Abelardo Galvis, in an interview, September 4, 1969.
28. Octavio Moreno, pastor of an Assemblies of God Church, in an interview, July 14, 1971.
29. Domingo Zuniga, in an interview, September 12, 1969.
30. Arthur Glasser, "The Propagation of Christianity," *Chuch Growth Bulletin,* 2 (Nov., 1965):1.
31. *Report on Baptist Church Growth in Colombia,* p. 40.
32. Melvin L. Hodges, *Mission—and Church Growth,* p. 3.
33. Dr. Wilbert Norton, "Mission—and Evaluating Methods," in *The Church's Worldwide Mission,* ed. Harold Lindsell, p. 186.
34. *Church Growth and Christian Mission,* ed. Donald McGavran, pp. 139-42.
35. Hodges, p. 11.
36. *Evangelism in Depth* (Chicago: Moody, 1961), p. 25.
37. *Church Growth and Christian Mission,* p. 117.
38. Hodges, p. 3.
39. Ibid., p. 10.
40. Ibid., p. 8.
41. Melvin Hodges, "Developing Basic Units in Indigenous Churches," in *Church Growth and Christian Mission,* p. 124.
42. Ibid.
43. C. Peter Wagner, "Faithful Men and Able to Teach: The Crisis in Ministerial Training in the Younger Churches" (mimeographed study, n.d.), pp. 7-8.
44. Ibid.
45. Melvin Hodges, "Workers' Training Program: Goals, Problems, and Methods," *Missionary Forum,* January-February, 1960, p. 8.
46. Hodges, "Developing Basic Units in Indigenous Churches," pp. 126-27.
47. Eugene Nida, "Communication of the Gospel in Latin America with Special Reference to Christian Literature and Radio," p. 10.
48. Ibid., p. 8.
49. Strachan, p. 10.

Selected Bibliography

BOOKS

Allen, Roland. *Missionary Methods, St. Paul's or Ours.* Grand Rapids: Eerdmans, 1962.

————. *The Spontaneous Expansion of the Church.* Grand Rapids: Eerdmans, 1962.

Barbieri, Sante Uberto. *Land of Eldorado.* New York: Friendship, 1961.

Bavinck, J. H. *An Introduction to the Science of Missions.* Grand Rapids: Baker, 1960.

Beyerhaus, Peter and Lefever, Henry. *The Responsible Church and the Foreign Mission.* Grand Rapids: Eerdmans, 1964.

Beyhaut, G. *Raices Contemporaneas de America Latina.* Buenos Aires: EUDEBA, 1964.

Bloch-Hoell, Nils. *The Pentecostal Movement.* Oslo, Norway: A/S, Halden, 1964.

Brumback, Carl. *God in Three Persons.* Cleveland, Tenn.: Pathway, 1959.

Calderon, L.; Calle, A.; and Dorselear, J. *Problemas de Urbanizacion en America Latina.* Bogota: FERES, 1963.

Chapman, Charles. *With the Bible Among the Andes.* Kansas City: GMU, n.d.

Considine, John J. *New Horizons in Latin America.* New York: Dodd, Mead, 1958.

Cook, Harold. *Strategy of Missions.* Chicago: Moody, 1961.

Corredor, B. and Torres, S. *Transformacion en el Mundo Rural Latinoamericano.* Bogota: FERES, 1961.

Damboriena, Prudencio. *El Protestantismo en America Latina.* 2 vols. Frieburg, Switz.: FERES, 1962-63.

D'Antonio, William and Pike, Fredrick. *Religion, Revolution, and Reform.* N.Y.: Frederick A. Praeger, 1964.

Davis, Merle J. *How the Church Grows in Brazil.* Concord, N. H.: Rumford, 1943.

Debuyst, F. *Las Clases Sociales en America Latina.* Bogota: FERES, 1962.

Frodsham, Stanley H. *With Signs Following.* Springfield, Mo.: Gospel Publishing, 1946.

Haddox, Benjamin E. *Sociedad y Religion en Colombia.* Bogota: Ediciones Tercer Mundo, 1965.

Hamill, Hugh M., Jr. *Dictatorship in Spanish America.* New York: Alfred A. Knopf, 1965.

Harper, M. *As at the Beginning: The Twentieth Century Pentecostal Revival.* London: Hodder & Stoughton, 1965.

Hodges, Melvin L. *Build My Church.* Springfield, Mo.: Foreign Missions Dept., Assemblies of God, 1957.

———. *Growing Young Churches.* Chicago: Moody, 1970.

Holt, Pat M. *Colombia Today—and Tomorrow.* New York: Frederick Praeger, 1964.

Hoover, W. C. *Historia del Avivamiento Pentecostal en Chile.* Valparaiso, Chile: Imp. Excelsior, 1948.

Kane, J. Herbert. *Twofold Growth.* Philadelphia: China Inland Mission, 1947.

Kendrick, Klaude. *The Promise Fulfilled.* Springfield, Mo.: Gospel Publishing, 1961.

Lalive d'Epinay, Christian. *El Refugio de las Masas: Estudio Sociologico del Protestantismo Chileno.* Santiago: Editorial Pacifico, 1968.

Lannoy, J. L. de. *Los Niveles de Vida en America Latina.* Bogota: FERES, 1963.

Latourette, Kenneth Scott. *Christianity in a Revolutionary Age.* 5 vols. New York: Harper & Row, 1962.

Lewis, Oscar. *Antropologia de la Pobreza.* Mexico: F. C. E., 1961.

———. *Los Hijos de Sanchez.* Mexico: Editorial J. Mortiz, 1965.

Lindsell, Harold. *A Christian Philosophy of Mission.* Wheaton: Van Kampen, 1949.

———, ed. *The Church's Worldwide Mission.* Waco, Tex.: Word, 1966.

Lopez, Francisco. *Proceso al Poder Religioso en Colombia.* Bogota: Editorial Evangelico de Colombia, 1966.

Luzbetak, Louis J. *The Church and Cultures.* Techny, Ill.: Divine Word, 1963.

Mackay, John A. *The Other Spanish Christ*. New York: Macmillan, 1932.

Mayer, F. E. *The Religious Bodies of America*. St. Louis, Mo.: Concordia, 1954.

McGavran, Donald. *Church Growth in Mexico*. Grand Rapids: Eerdmans, 1963.

————. *How Churches Grow*. London: World Dominion, 1959.

————. *The Bridges of God*. New York: Friendship, 1955.

————, ed. *Church Growth and Christian Mission*. New York: Harper & Row, 1965.

Mead, Frank S. *Handbook of Denominations*. Nashville: Abingdon, 1956.

Nehemkis, Peter. *Latin America, Myth and Reality*. New York: New Amer. Lib., 1966.

Neill, Stephen and Weber, Hans-Ruedi. *The Layman in Christian History*. London: SCM, 1963.

Neve, J. L. *Churches and Sects of Christendom*. Burlington, Iowa: Lutheran Lit. Board, 1940.

Nichol, John T. *Pentecostalism*. New York: Harper & Row, 1966.

Nida, Eugene A. *Message and Mission*. New York: Harper & Row, 1960.

Niebuhr, H. R. *The Social Sources of Denominationalism*. New York: Holt, 1920.

Obermiller, Rudolf. *Evangelism in Latin America*. London: Lutterworth, 1957.

Ordonez, Francisco. *Historia del Cristianismo Evangelico en Colombia*. Medellin, Colombia: Tipografia Union, n.d.

Paulk, Earl P., Jr. *Your Pentecostal Neighbor*. Cleveland, Tenn.: Pathway, 1958.

Perez, Gustavo and Wust, Isaac. *La Iglesia en Colombia*. Frieburg, Switz.: FERES, 1961.

Pin, E. *Elementos para una Sociologia del Catolicismo Latinoamericano*. Bogota: FERES, 1963.

Plath, O. *Folklore Religioso Chileno*. Santiago: PlaTur, 1966.

Read, William R. *New Patterns of Church Growth in Brazil*. Grand Rapids: Eerdmans, 1965.

Read, William R.; Monterroso, V. M.; and Johnson, H. A. *Latin American Church Growth*. Grand Rapids: Eerdmans, 1969.

Sherill, J. L. *They Speak with Other Tongues*. London: Hodder & Stoughton, 1965.

Taylor, Clyde and Coffins, Wade. *Protestant Missions in Latin America: A Statistical Survey.* Washington, D. C.: EFMA, 1961.

Vergara, Ignacio. *El Protestantismo en Chile.* 2d ed. Santiago: Editorial del Pacifico, 1962.

Wach, J. *Sociology of Religion.* Chicago: U. Chicago, 1964.

Wilson, B. R. *Sects and Society.* London: Heinemann, 1961.

Winter, Ralph D., ed. *Theological Education by Extension.* S. Pasadena, Cal.: William Carey Lib., 1969.

Wood, William W. *Culture and Personality Aspects of the Pentecostal Holiness Religion.* Paris: Mouton, 1965.

Yinger, J. M. *Religion, Society, Individual.* New York: Macmillan, 1957.

ARTICLES

Castro, Emilio. "Evangelism in Latin America." *International Review of Missions* 8 (Oct. 1964):452-56.

"Facts of a Field: Colombia." *World Vision Magazine,* April 1971, p. 22.

Hodges, Melvin L. "Spiritual Dynamics in El Salvador." *Evangelical Missions Quarterly* 2(Winter 1966):80-83.

———. "Workers' Training Program: Goals, Problems, and Methods." *Missionary Forum,* January-February 1960, p. 8.

Hoeferkamp, Robert T. "Our Message and Environment." *Lutheran World* 9 (July 1962):235-42.

Holt, John B. "Holiness Religion: Cultural Shock and Social Reorganization." *American Sociological Review* 5 (Oct. 1940): 740.

Johnson, B. "Do Holiness Sects Socialize Dominant Values?" *Social Forces* 39 (May 1961):309-16.

McGavran, Donald. "Mission Evaluated by Experts." *Church Growth Bulletin* 3 (Sept. 1966):7-8.

Nida, Eugene. "Communication of the Gospel to Latin Americans." *Practical Anthropology* 8 (July-Aug. 1961):145-56.

———. "Kerygma and Culture: Underlying Problems in Communication of the Gospel in Spanish-speaking Latin America." *Lutheran World* 8 (Dec. 1961):269-80.

———. "The Indigenous Churches in Latin America." *Practical Anthropology* 8 (May-June 1961):97-105.

Poblete, Renalto and Odea, Thomas F. "Anomie and the 'Quest for Community': The Formation of the Sects Among Puerto Ricans of New York." *The American Catholic Sociological Review* 21 (Spring 1960):18-36.

Renshaw, Parke. "A New Religion for Brazilians." *Practical Anthropology* 13 (July-Aug. 1966): 126-32.

Snyder, Charles S., Jr. "Pentecostals." *The Missionary Messenger,* Sept. 1969, pp. 20-21.

Strachan, Kenneth. "Call to Witness." *International Review of Missions* 53 (Apr. 1964):191-200.

Strunk, Leon E. "A Chief Key to Church Growth." *Church Growth Bulletin* 3 (Nov. 1966): 7-8.

Tippett, Alan R. "Biblical Basis of Church Growth." *Church Growth Bulletin* 3 (Jan. 1967):2-3.

Walker, Louise J. "Stepping Up the Training Program." *Key: For Key People in Key Places* 13 (January-March 1965):11-12.

"Why Some Churches Grow Spectacularly—and Others Don't." *Latin American Evangelist,* May-June 1967, pp. 8-9.

REPORTS

Goff, James E. *Censo de la Obra Evangelica en Colombia: 1966.* Bogota: CEDEC, 1966.

———. *Census of Protestant Church Members in Colombia: 1968.* Bogota: CEDEC, 1969.

———. *Census of Protestant Church Members in Colombia: 1969.* Bogota: CEDEC, 1969.

Hodges, Melvin L. *Mission—and Church Growth.* Wheaton Study Papers: Congress on the Church's Worldwide Mission, 1966.

Report on Baptist Church Growth in Colombia. Cali: Southern Baptist Mission of Colombia, 1968.

Strachan, Kenneth. *The Missionary Movement of the Non-Historical Groups in Latin America.* New York: CCLA, 1957.

UNPUBLISHED MATERIAL

Flora, Cornelia. "History of the United Pentecostal Church in Colombia." A mimeographed study in preparation for her dissertation, n.d.

DENOMINATIONAL TRACTS, PUBLICATIONS

Bodas de Plata. Medellin: Multigraficas, 1967.

Constitucion. Bogota: Concilio de las Asambleas de Dios de Colombia, mimeo, n.d.

Manual: Articulos de Fe y Constitucion. Pereira: Editorial Sigma, 1967.

Manual de Doctrina y Practica Cristianas (Reglamento Local). Bogota: Tipografia Hispana, n.d.

Stevens, Roberto. *Los Primeros Rudimentos.* Bogota: Editorial "Buena Semilla," 1959.

Vouga, Oscar. "Nuestro Mensaje Evangelico." United Pentecostal Church, n.d.